GOLD experience
2ND EDITION

WORKBOOK

B1
Preliminary
for Schools

CONTENTS

Listening	Speaking	Writing	Review
topic: places in town **task:** multiple choice	**topic:** giving personal information **task:** introductions – social interaction	**topic:** school councils **task:** email	unit check 1
topic: app camp **task:** sentence completion	**topic:** communicating **task:** describing a photo	**topic:** not such a great evening **task:** story	unit check 2
topic: technology and entertainment **task:** multiple choice (pictures)	**topic:** technology and entertainment **task:** collaborative task and discussion	**topic:** making a big purchase **task:** email	unit check 3 review: units 1–3 (p30)
topic: training to be a gymnast **task:** multiple choice	**topic:** dangerous sports **task:** describing a photo	**topic:** sports at and outside school **task:** article	unit check 4
topic: music **task:** multiple choice	**topic:** playing music **task:** describing a photo	**topic:** favourite music **task:** article	unit check 5
topic: a local event to help the environment **task:** multiple choice	**topic:** reducing plastic waste **task:** collaborative task	**topic:** visiting a friend **task:** email	unit check 6 review: units 1–6 (p56)
topic: an online travel show **task:** sentence completion	**topic:** going on holiday **task:** discussion	**topic:** travel tips **task:** article	unit check 7
topic: hobbies **task:** multiple choice (pictures)	**topic:** learning a new skill **task:** collaborative task	**topic:** hobbies **task:** article	unit check 8
topic: experiences **task:** multiple choice	**topic:** weekend activities **task:** collaborative task and discussion	**topic:** an unforgettable experience **task:** story	unit check 9 review: units 1–9 (p82)

Starter   Happy days

1 Match sentence halves (1–7) and (A–G).

1 This summer I travelled ....
2 On the first day we looked ....
3 After that we went ....
4 I tried ....
5 Then we met ....
6 I didn't take any ....
7 We didn't want to return ....

A around the British Museum for hours.
B British food and I liked it.
C home because we were having such a good time.
D to London with my parents.
E photos of the palace because there were too many people.
F walking along the river Thames.
G some friends from home, outside Buckingham Palace!

2 Choose the adjective which has a similar meaning to the word in brackets, to complete each sentence.

amazing   boring   gorgeous   huge   successful

1 Their first performance was .... (very good) .
2 Let me show you a photo of my .... (very pretty) dog!
3 I liked the book, but the film was really .... (not very interesting).
4 The city centre isn't .... (very big), but there's lots to do.
5 My cousin's a .... (top) businesswoman. She owns a technology company.

3 Write the word that completes all three sentences in each group.

1 If you do well in the competition, you will get a …
   For my last project, my teacher gave me a …
   My favourite team has won first …
   p...........................

2 I'm really tired – I need a …
   You have a busy day tomorrow – try to get some …
   After carrying the boxes upstairs, we stopped for a …
   r...........................

3 I'm pleased to be learning a new …
   For me, cooking isn't a hobby; it's a …
   A great footballer needs both speed and …
   s...........................

4 Travelling to Australia takes a long …
   I love the weekends because I have lots of free …
   I'm going to swim outdoors for the first …
   t...........................

5 Everyone clapped when the actor walked onto the …
   I get nervous every time I'm on …
   She sang her song, said goodnight and left the …
   s...........................

4 Choose the correct words to complete the message.

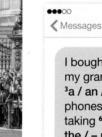

●●○○ 🔋 📶 ⤴ ⬚ 🔋
‹ Messages   Details

I bought (a)/ the / – new phone on Saturday. I used ¹a / the / – money my grandparents gave me for my birthday. ²A / The / – phone has ³a / an / the amazing camera, of course. You know I love ⁴a / the / – phones with ⁵a / the / – good cameras! My mum always says, 'Stop taking ⁶a / the / – photos of life and just live it!' But I think that ⁷a / the / – photography is ⁸a / an / – useful skill and also ⁹a / an / the interesting hobby. And who knows, I might even be ¹⁰a / the / – famous photographer one day!

5 Complete the article with a, an, the or no article (–).

TOP TEN
foods to try while you're in
MEXICO

① Elote

Elote is a very popular snack and you shouldn't leave ¹........ Mexico without trying it. It's made from grilled corn with ²........ salt, chilli, lime, butter and cheese. You can eat elote from ³........ cup, but it's easier to eat it on ⁴........ stick – rather like ⁵........ ice cream. You'll find it at ⁶........ most cafés or restaurants in tourist areas, but ⁷........ best place to buy it is in ⁸........ street, cooked on a barbecue.

6 Make sentences using the comparative form of the adjectives in brackets.

1 dogs / cats (friendly)

....

2 cycling to school / taking the bus (good)

....

3 trying new foods / always eating the same things (interesting)

....

....

4 the food market / the supermarket (cheap)

....

5 summers in Spain / summers in the UK (hot)

....

....

6 having a picnic / cooking a meal (easy)

....

....

7 Complete the sentences with the superlative form of the adjectives in brackets.

1 Mexico City is .... (big) city I've visited.

2 Walking is .... (natural) way to get fit.

3 Yuk! That's .... (bad) cup of coffee I've ever had.

4 Yesterday was .... (happy) day of my life.

5 The paintings inside that building are .... (beautiful) ones in Rome.

6 Finishing my project was .... (good) feeling ever!

8 Rewrite the sentences using (not) as … as.

1 Having a picnic is more interesting than eating indoors.

....

....

2 My brother is more active than me.

....

....

3 Kelly is very shy and so is Amanda.

....

....

4 Doing your best is more important than winning.

....

....

5 Pete was very disappointed and so was Eric.

....

....

9 🔊 S.1 Complete the conversation with these verbs. There are three extra verbs which you do not need. Listen and check your answers.

be	couldn't	did	do	fell	had	was	wasn't
		went	were	weren't			

A: Hi! Did you have a good weekend?

B: Yes, I **1**........................ , thanks. I **2**........................ horse-riding for the first time.

A: Wow! Where did you **3**........................ that?

B: In the countryside near my uncle's village. It **4**........................ amazing! I **5**........................ to wear a special helmet and riding boots.

A: I'd love to try horse-riding. But it sounds a bit scary!

B: It's not. Well, at least I **6**........................ scared – I was on the horse with my uncle. Although I nearly **7**........................ off the horse at one point! It wanted to run but, luckily, my uncle was in control, so it **8**........................ go too fast.

10 When was the last time you did these things? Write true sentences about you using the past simple. Use when where possible.

1 try a new food

....

2 take a photo

....

3 have a meal with a friend / friends

....

4 swim in the sea or a lake

....

5 travel by train

....

6 buy something

....

1 Identity

READING

1 Complete the text with these words and phrases.

background   hang out with   sticker   taking part   valley

This is a photo of me with my walking club. Here we're all ¹............................ in a hike for charity. It's something we do once a year. We hike every weekend for two months, and collect a ²............................ each time. I think we're doing the second hike in this photo. We're walking across a bridge. You can't see it but there's a deep ³............................ under the bridge and we were really high up. In the ⁴............................ you can see the woods we were walking through. The bridge was so high up, we were near the tops of the trees!

We don't always go for long walks in the group. Sometimes we just meet to ⁵............................ each other and have fun.

2 Read about five people who are looking for a club to join. Answer the questions.

Who:

1 wants to get better at their hobby?   ....
2 is interested in technology?   ....
3 is already very good at their hobby?   ....
4 enjoys wearing costumes?   ....
5 is new to the area?   ....

3 e Read the advertisements for eight clubs. Decide which club (A–H) would be the most suitable for each person (1–5).

1 Callum ....   3 Tom ....   5 Chris ....
2 Elena ....   4 Sarah ....

---

1 Callum

I love computers. I spend a lot of time programming my own PC and trying out new games. I also enjoy solving puzzles and problems.

2 Elena

I moved here a couple of months ago and I'd like to find a new hobby and also meet local teenagers. I love being outside and I like most sports, but I don't like competitions.

3 Tom

I was a member of a club last year but I didn't learn as much as I wanted to. I like making things and I draw pictures all the time. I want to have fun, but I'm also interested in studying a bit, so I can improve.

4 Sarah

In my free time I do experiments with my 'home lab' kit. Last year I won the Young Einstein prize at my school. I want to study Biochemistry at university and I'd like to meet young people who like the same things as me.

5 Chris

I have a good imagination and I'd love to find a hobby to inspire me. I enjoy acting and drama. I like dressing up and playing the part of someone different from myself. I'm thinking about being an actor when I leave school.

A We've set up the Film Club for everyone who loves movies. We show a film every Friday afternoon, 4–6 p.m., in the hall. We also get together on the first Saturday of each month to go to the cinema in town, and have pizza afterwards.

B Do you love finding out about how the world works? Then come and feed your hungry mind at the Vector Club. We welcome visitors to talk to us about careers in science, we organise science workshops and we often send a team to competitions. Ask Peter Stevens in Class 8B for more details.

C The Badminton Club meets in the sports hall every Thursday after school. You need to be at intermediate level to get the most out of our sessions. You can sign up for the club by visiting our page on the school website and following the 'New member' link.

D **Roleplay** is a great way to make friends. We organise fantasy and strategy games for people who love to escape from the everyday. Come along and be someone else for a couple of hours – costumes are optional! We meet in the rec room on Fridays at 3.30 p.m.

E The Baseball Club is a friendly group of young people who meet to get fit and hang out. We play our matches at the local park on Sundays and then we have a picnic or a barbecue. Come and join in – our club is not about winning, it's about having fun!

F **Why not take up painting?** You can express yourself and meet people like you. We have members of all levels and abilities and we spend as much time painting outdoors as we can. Contact Zoe in Class 8A for more information.

G If you live in the digital world, you'll love our Tech Club. We don't just sit around looking at screens and playing all day, you know! We're looking forward to a trip to the Technology Exhibition next month. Visit our website for details.

H **The Art Club**

The Art Club meets once a month on a Saturday morning. Each session is about a different subject and we usually have a presentation by a local artist or art teacher. We also organise visits to art galleries to learn from the masters. Contact details below.

4 Match the phrasal verbs (1–7) from the advertisements in Ex 3 with their meanings (A–G).

1 set up ....
2 get together ....
3 find out (about) ....
4 sign up (for) ....
5 join in ....
6 take up ....
7 look forward to ....

A take part
B start doing a new activity
C feel excited about something that is going to happen
D start a new club, organisation or company
E get more information on
F put your name on a list for something because you want to take part in it
G meet each other

5 Complete the sentences with phrasal verbs from Ex 4.

1 I need to buy a racket because I'm going to .... tennis.
2 Ed and Joe never .... when we play football. They just watch.
3 There aren't any youth clubs in my town, so we're going to .... a new one.
4 I always .... the end-of-year competition. I love taking part and I usually win, too!
5 I'd like to join your group. Where can I .... it?
6 I'm not sure I would like climbing. I have to .... it before I decide.
7 Shall we .... at the weekend to go shopping for new clothes?

GRAMMAR

present simple and present continuous

1 Complete the sentences with the present simple or present continuous form of these verbs. Use the same verb for both gaps.

eat   listen   play   snow   study   tidy   watch   wear

1 We usually .... volleyball but at the moment we .... basketball.

2 Today she .... jeans, but most of the time she .... a skirt.

3 I often .... cereal for breakfast, but this morning I .... toast.

4 Today Peter .... to the radio, although he usually .... to music on his MP3 player.

5 We .... tennis from Wimbledon on the TV now. We .... it every year.

6 That's strange – look, it .... outside. It never .... in June!

7 My sister .... her room at the moment – she only .... it once a week.

8 My friends and I often .... together but today we .... on our own.

2 Complete the questions to a friend. Use *you* and the present simple or present continuous form of the verbs in brackets.

1 What .... (listen) to? It sounds like a group that I know.

2 You look worried. What .... (think) about?

3 .... (understand) the homework? Can you explain it to me?

4 Are you reading the new Elena Rose book? What .... (think) of it?

5 Why .... (talk) to me that way? Are you upset?

6 .... (often / listen) to classical music?

7 I'm not sure I understand. What .... (mean)?

8 What's Madrid like? .... (have) a good time?

3 🔊 1.1 Listen to Jess talking to her best friend Amelia. Answer the questions. Write full sentences in the present simple or present continuous.

1 Where do Jess's aunt and uncle live?

....

2 What's the weather like in Manchester?

....

3 What is Jess doing?

....

4 Where do Jess and her aunt and uncle sometimes go in the evenings?

....

5 How does Amelia feel?

....

6 Why does Amelia have to go?

....

4 🔊 1.2 Choose the correct verb forms to complete the sentences from the recording. Listen again and check your answers.

1 It **seems / is seeming** as if you're in the next room.

2 **Do you joke / Are you joking**? It's completely different here.

3 I **don't believe / am not believing** it!

4 They **build / are building** a swimming pool now.

5 We **hear / are hearing** them all the time in the garden.

6 Hang on a minute – I **hold / am holding** the phone out now.

7 They **don't sound / aren't sounding** like British birds at all!

8 He **makes / is making** breakfast this morning.

5 Complete the text with the present simple or present continuous form of the verbs in brackets.

Young chefs

Antonio comes from Brazil, but at the moment he
[1] .... (visit) his aunt in Brighton. He [2] .... (stay) with his English aunt for the school holidays. He
[3] .... (like) his aunt very much, so today he [4] .... (want) to cook dinner for her.

Antonio says:

'English food [5] .... (taste) very different from the food back home. To be honest, I think it is a bit boring. So today I [6] .... (make) a traditional Brazilian meal for my aunt to try. I [7] .... (use) a recipe I found on the internet. It [8] .... (look) good in the photos, so let's hope she likes it!'

VOCABULARY

personality adjectives

1 Match these words with the pictures (1–6).

calm   clever   lazy   noisy   shy   sporty

1 ....

2 ....

3 ....

4 ....

5 ....

6 ....

2 Match the sentences (1–6) with the descriptions (A–F).

1 Lisa doesn't mind speaking in public.

2 Diane tells everyone what to do.

3 Leila never says 'please' or 'thank you'.

4 Grace makes me laugh.

5 Tia doesn't often joke or smile.

6 Sophie is always busy and fun to be with.

A She's funny.

B She's lively.

C She's serious.

D She's confident.

E She's bossy.

F She's rude.

3 Complete the conversations with adjectives from Exs 1 and 2.

1 A: I think I'm going to fail the exam.

   B: No, you're not – you study a lot. You should be more .... !

2 A: I'm spending the day playing computer games.

   B: Oh you're so .... ! You need to get more exercise!

3 A: I don't really want to meet your friends at the party.

   B: Don't be .... Try to talk more and you'll be fine.

4 A: Your new coat is really ugly.

   B: Hey! That's very .... Say 'sorry'!

5 A: That's the funniest thing I've ever heard!

   B: Can you stop laughing and be .... for a moment? This is important!

6 A: Let's get together at the weekend and play some football.

   B: You know I'm not very .... – I'd rather stay at home and watch TV.

4 Read what twin brothers say about each other and choose the correct prepositions.

My brother and I look similar, but our personalities are quite different. I'm not very good **¹in / at** talking to people I don't know and I'm frightened **²with / of** going to new places. Jorge is much better **³at / about** making friends.

Sergio is a bit shy, but he's brilliant **⁴at / in** listening and he's very clever. I sometimes get fed up **⁵about / with** him because he knows all the answers at school! We like the same things, though. We're both keen **⁶with / on** football and we're interested **⁷in / on** technology and computers.

5 Complete the sentences about you. Use one of these prepositions in each sentence.

about   at (x2)   in   of   with

1 I'm bored ....

2 I'm interested ....

3 I'm excited ....

4 I'm frightened ....

5 I'm brilliant ....

6 I'm bad ....

Extend

6 Complete the definitions with these words.

anxious   brave   careless   polite   reliable   sociable

1 A(n) .... person worries about things.

2 A(n) .... person always keeps promises.

3 A(n) .... person makes a lot of mistakes.

4 A(n) .... person likes spending time with other people.

5 A(n) .... person can help others in a dangerous situation.

6 A(n) .... person respects other people and speaks kindly.

7 🔊 1.3 Listen to a teacher talking about students. Match the names (1–6) with the descriptions (A–F) to make sentences.

1 Fran

2 Sam

3 Clare

4 Alex

5 Isobel

6 Nick

A is careless with school work.

B is anxious about exams.

C was brave during the school trip.

D isn't very polite to the teachers.

E is reliable.

F needs to be less sociable in class.

1 Identity

LISTENING

1 Read questions (1–6) and highlight the key words. The first one is done for you.

1 You will hear two friends talking about what to do next in a museum. What are they going to look at?

   A some coins

   B some paintings

   C souvenirs they can buy

2 You will hear two friends talking about travelling by bus. How does the boy feel about it?

   A worried

   B excited

   C fed up

3 You will hear two friends who are shopping for clothes. What does the girl think her friend should do?

   A get a different size

   B choose a darker colour

   C try a more modern style

4 You will hear two friends trying to find their way in a shopping centre. What does the boy think they should do?

   A use an electronic map

   B go to the information desk

   C take the lift rather than the stairs

5 You will hear two friends choosing a film to see. Which type of film do they both like?

   A comedy

   B action

   C science fiction

6 You will hear two friends talking about a café they often go to. Which opinion do they share?

   A The café looks better than it did before.

   B The quality of the food is the most important thing.

   C They don't like the new furniture.

2 Look at the questions in Ex 1 again and the key words you highlighted. Decide if you are listening for an agreement (A), a suggestion (S) or feelings (F) in each question.

1 ....   **3** ....   **5** ....

2 ....   **4** ....   **6** ....

3 e ◀)) 1.4 Listen to the six different conversations from Ex 1. For each question, choose the correct answer.

adverbs of frequency, time phrases

4 Match these adverbs or time phrases with those with a similar meaning below (1–6).

every day	frequently	hardly ever	most days	now and then	once a month

1 occasionally ....   **4** always ....

2 rarely ....   **5** every four weeks ....

3 usually ....   **6** often ....

5 Rewrite the sentences. Put the adverb or time phrase in brackets in the correct place.

1 My parents go to the cinema. (hardly ever)

....

2 We don't eat at restaurants because my brother is too little. (often)

....

3 Is the museum closed on Sundays? (always)

....

4 I find my way without using a map. (usually)

....

5 I don't go to the city centre. (on weekdays)

....

6 We travel by train. (rarely)

....

6 Write true sentences about you. They can be positive or negative.

1 take the bus / often

....

2 meet my friends after school / every day

....

3 go to the same café / always

....

4 choose my own clothes in shops / usually

....

5 be late for school / all the time

....

6 get lost / often

....

SPEAKING

1 Put the words in the correct order to make questions.

1 your / what / surname / 's?

What's your surname?

2 middle / 's / your / what / name?

....

....

3 address / your / 's / what?

....

....

4 town / how / of / the / the / do / spell / you / name?

....

....

5 what / postcode / your / 's?

....

....

6 please / your / can / email / spell / address, / you?

....

....

2 🔊 1.5 Read the form. Listen to a girl called Sophie answering the questions in Ex1 and complete the form.

NEW MEMBER FORM	
Full name:	
Address:	
Town:	
Postcode:	
Email address:	

3 🔊 1.6 Listen to the questions again and answer about yourself. Listen to your recording to see how clear your answers were.

4 Complete the questions with *what, where, who* or *how.*

1 .... do you come from?

2 .... do you like doing in your free time?

3 ....'s your favourite subject?

4 .... do you get to school every day?

5 .... cooks your meals at home?

6 .... helps you to buy your clothes?

5 Choose the correct words to complete the answers. Then match the answers (A–F) with the questions in Ex 4 (1–6).

A I love playing chess. One **example / reason** I like it is because it makes me think. ....

B My mum or dad, but I sometimes cook simple meals too – **for / so** example, pasta with sauce. ....

C My favourite subject's science **because / so** I like doing lots of different experiments. ....

D I'm from Warsaw, the capital of Poland. There are lots of good things about living there – for **example / reason**, there are lots of shops and restaurants. ....

E My sister and I like the same things, **because / so** I usually ask her to help me. ....

F My mum drives me to school **because / so** she passes my school on her way to work. ....

6 Read part of an interview with a student. Complete his answers with these words.

also   because   but   for example   one reason   so

Q: Where do you live?

A: I'm from Odessa. It's a big city in Ukraine, **1**......................... it's not the capital.

Q: And what's your favourite thing about living there?

A: Well, **2**......................... I love Odessa is because it's a beautiful city. There are some amazing buildings – **3**........................., the Opera and Ballet Theatre.

Q: Do you live with your family?

A: Yes – with my parents and my two brothers. I get on well with my brothers and I enjoy spending time with them. Maybe it's **4**......................... we like doing the same things.

Q: What do you like doing in the summer?

A: We all enjoy water sports, **5**......................... we go canoeing or swimming in the sea.

Q: What about in the winter?

A: In the winter we **6**......................... go to the sea, but we go for long walks along the beach.

7 🔊 1.7 Listen and check your answers. Then answer the questions from the conversation in Ex 6 about yourself.

11

1 Identity

WRITING

an email

1 Read these sentences from different students' emails. Decide if they are about personality (P), hobbies (H) or likes and dislikes (LD).

1 I'd say my sister is very calm. ....
2 I can't stand computer games. ....
3 My brother and I go skateboarding at the weekend. ....
4 I'm keen on cats, dogs, rabbits – any kind of animal. ....
5 I love travelling to new places. ....
6 My grandmother is sixty now, but she's really lively. ....
7 I do karate once a week. ....

2 Match these adjectives with the prepositions we use them with. Write them in the correct column in the table.

bored brilliant fed up good interested keen terrible

at	with	on	in
brilliant			

3 Complete the second sentence so it means the same as the first. Use these words and the words in brackets.

bossy interested keen scared serious shy sporty

1 I like reading fantasy novels. (quite)
I'm .... on reading fantasy novels.
2 I don't smile a lot. (quite)
I'm .... person.
3 I don't often tell people what to do. (very)
I'm not a .... person.
4 I'm terrified of heights. (very)
I'm .... of heights.
5 Learning to speak German interests me. (quite)
I'm .... in learning to speak German.
6 I find it hard to talk to people I don't know. (very)
I'm .... around people I don't know.

4 Read the advert from a school website and notes 1–4. Answer the questions.

1 What kind of text do you need to write? ....
2 How many things do you need to write about? What are they?
....
....

Elections for the school council

School councils represent the views of students, so they're really important. This year there will be two representatives for each class. If you think you could be one of them, tell your classmates!

Write them an email saying what you're like. What's the best thing about you? What are you good at? Tell the class why they should choose you!

1 write about my personality
2 tell them
3 say what
4 give a reason

5 Read Ed's email and answer the questions.

Dear Classmates,

I'm Ed Anderson and I want to be your school councillor.

I'm quite a serious person, but I'm also friendly. You can talk to me if you have any problems at school. My friends say the best thing about me is that I always try to help people when I can.

I'm very good at speaking in public and I'm also good at listening. That's another reason I'm the right person for this job.

You should choose me because I want to help the school and I have lots of good ideas. I promise I'll make our school better.

I hope you will vote for me!

Ed

1 Does he write about all the points? ....
2 Does he give extra information about each point? ....
3 Does he use adjectives? Find examples.
....
4 What two words does he use to make adjectives stronger or less strong?
....

6 e Read the advert in Ex 4 again and write your own email in about 100 words. Use your answers to Exs 4 and 5 and Ed's email to help you.

UNIT CHECK

1 Complete the blog post with the correct form of the verbs in brackets.

I'm Besim. I usually ¹............................ (speak) Turkish at home, but today I ²............................ (speak) English, because my friend William from England ³............................ (stay) with me at the moment. He ⁴............................ (come) to school with me every day.

William has just started learning Turkish, so there are a lot of words he ⁵............................ (not know). He ⁶............................ (not understand) me and my friends when we chat. I have to translate for him. My English ⁷............................ (improve), but his Turkish ⁸............................ (not get) better!

2 Make questions about the text in Ex 1. Use the present simple or present continuous.

1 what language / Besim / usually / speak at home?

....

2 why / he / speak / English / today?

....

3 where / Besim and William / go every day?

....

4 why / Besim / have to / translate for William?

....

5 William's Turkish / improve?

....

3 Answer the questions in Ex 2. Write full sentences.

4 Read the clues and complete the puzzle with personality adjectives. Then guess the mystery adjective and complete the clue.

1 intelligent
2 not calm
3 not funny
4 not reliable
5 not rude
mystery adjective:
.... =
not ....

5 e Read the article. For each question, choose the correct answer.

Maybe my parents are right …

Are you fed up ¹........ your parents asking you to switch off your phone? So am I! But I understand why parents are unhappy – our social lives are very different ²........ theirs and they're worried. They think we're all bad ³........ writing and terrible ⁴........ communicating face to face. I don't think that's true, but maybe we should be hanging out ⁵........ our friends more and taking part ⁶........ activities. My parents say we spend a lot less time outdoors than they did, and I think they're probably right.

1	(A) with	B	at	C	for
2	A of	B	that	C	from
3	A at	B	with	C	in
4	A in	B	for	C	at
5	A to	B	with	C	about
6	A on	B	in	C	from

6 e Read the blog post and write the correct answers. Write one word for each gap.

About school …

I'm so bored ¹............................ homework! I spend two hours doing it most days and I have to complete a project ²............................ weekend. That's fifty-two projects a year! Anyway, at least it was a good day at school today because I had drama. I'm really keen ³............................ drama, but we only have it ⁴............................ a week, on Friday afternoons. I'm always really happy on Fridays!

The drama group puts on a play twice a year – in December and June. We usually perform a classical play, but now and ⁵............................ we write our own play. This year I ⁶............................ helping and I'm very excited about it!

READING

1 Put the letters in brackets in order to form a word which completes each sentence. The first letter of each new word is in bold.

1 Stop playing on your phone and pay .... (tenoni**a**tt) to what I'm saying!

2 People around the world speak English – it's an .... (tiatneln**r**aino) language.

3 Jeans with holes in them are very .... (abashole**f**in) these days.

4 Unfortunately, languages .... (a**d**ispapre) all the time – people simply stop speaking them.

5 The national language here is Spanish, but many .... (l**c**aol) people also speak German.

6 At first I didn't .... (**s**reeail) that she was Italian, but then I read an article about her.

7 An .... (ar**i**scening) number of people are learning languages online each year.

8 Learning a foreign language will .... (l**a**lwo) you to communicate with more people.

2 Match the responses (A–H) with the sentences (1–8) above.

A It's true, but we can try to change that by teaching young people about them. ....

B Definitely – English is unique in that sense. ....

C Oh really? What was it about? ....

D Those people are lucky to grow up speaking two useful languages. ....

E That's right – speaking another language makes both travelling and business much easier. ....

F Sorry, I'm listening now. ....

G Maybe, but it doesn't mean that they look good! ....

H Using technology is a great way to learn. ....

3 **e** Read the notices and the emails (1–3). For each question, choose the correct answer.

① Wanted: second-hand violin for learner aged 8–12. Willing to pay up to £80, more for an instrument in excellent condition.

A The buyer is looking for a violin that costs £80.

B The buyer might be happy to spend more than £80.

C The buyer will only spend £80 or less.

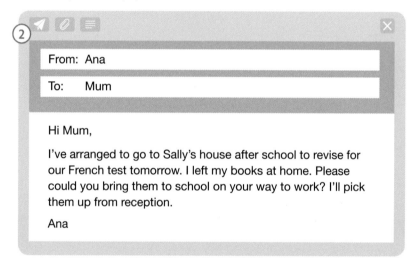

②

From: Ana

To: Mum

Hi Mum,

I've arranged to go to Sally's house after school to revise for our French test tomorrow. I left my books at home. Please could you bring them to school on your way to work? I'll pick them up from reception.

Ana

A Ana wants her mum to take something to Sally's house.

B Ana would like her mum to collect her from Sally's house.

C Ana asks her mum to deliver something to her.

③ If you'd like to go on next month's Spanish language exchange trip, write your name here. You must get permission from your parents before registering, even if you have been on previous trips.

A It's the parents' job to register their children for the trip.

B All students must ask their parents before they sign up.

C Only students who have been on a trip before can attend.

4 Read the article about language quickly. Does the writer think emoji language is generally positive or negative?

5 🅔 Read the article again. For each question, choose the correct answer.

1 In the first paragraph, the writer says that emojis
- **A** make conversation between people better.
- **B** encourage understanding between cultures.
- **C** persuade more people to text.
- **D** are a new language.

2 How does the writer think emojis affect written language?
- **A** Not everyone knows what the emojis mean.
- **B** They make messages unclear.
- **C** People are unable to explain things clearly.
- **D** There is too much focus on images, not words.

3 According to the writer, spelling tools on our mobile phones
- **A** make bad predictions about what we'd like to write.
- **B** are a benefit to teachers.
- **C** help people to use punctuation correctly.
- **D** stop young people from using their brains.

4 What does the writer say about emojis in school work?
- **A** They make students appear bad at writing.
- **B** They can cause confusion.
- **C** They bring in unnecessary feelings.
- **D** They make young people lazy.

5 Which sentence best describes how the writer feels about emojis?
- **A** Emojis are a good way for us to avoid learning to spell.
- **B** Young people need to learn to write without emojis.
- **C** Social networks should stop using emojis.
- **D** Emojis can help create international friendships.

6 Find these words in the article. Then choose the correct meaning for each word as it appears in the article.

1 achieved (para 1)
- **A** succeeded in doing
- **B** failed

2 communicate (para 2)
- **A** chat
- **B** make people understand

3 bother (para 3)
- **A** annoy someone
- **B** make the effort to do something

4 effect (para 3)
- **A** result
- **B** advantage

5 mood (para 4)
- **A** the way we act
- **B** the way we feel

6 weak (para 4)
- **A** not good
- **B** not having much energy

A new world language

Shigetaka Kurita first created emojis while working for a mobile phone company. He wanted to design pictures that improved short text messages by making them sound friendlier, an aim he certainly achieved. Emojis weren't very popular when I was growing up but today they're like a world language. In fact, some people say emojis are the fastest-growing language.

A written language that uses pictures isn't new. The Egyptians had one, for example. However, it's worrying that emojis are so popular. I developed a large vocabulary while I was learning English at school. That vocabulary helps me to communicate a lot of different, difficult ideas in a way that people understand. If we use emojis all the time, we lose the ability to write. We can only communicate ideas in simple ways in texts.

Of course, it's normal for language to change over time and it's great that the written form continues today online. However, we spend a lot of time writing only short messages and using technology that guesses the word we want to type. It also changes spelling mistakes, so no one needs to learn how to spell any more. As well as that, no one seems to bother with punctuation. Teachers can see the effect of this in written work in the classroom.

The ability to write well is important for our school lives. Using emojis is a good way to show our mood quickly, and they are fine to use with friends but using them in school work is a bad idea. It just makes the writer seem like a weak communicator. Writing is a key skill in education. Teachers need to make sure that young people can all write well so that they can communicate well. This means learning to write without emojis and understanding when they are and aren't OK.

15

GRAMMAR

past simple and past continuous

1 Complete the table with past simple form of the verbs.

infinitive	past simple
carry	
come	
have	
hear	
move	
plan	
study	
win	

2 Read the sentences (1–8) about what different people were doing last night. Complete the sentences with the past continuous form of the verbs in brackets.

1 I .... (chat) to my friend Ali on my phone.

2 We .... (learn) some new English words. We .... (not do) a great job, though!

3 I was with my sister. We .... (have) dinner and, for once, we .... (not argue)!

4 It .... (rain) and I .... (stand) at the bus stop getting wet.

5 My brother .... (tell) me about something but I .... (not listen)!

6 My friend and I .... (watch) a film. I .... (not enjoy) it very much.

7 I .... (talk) to my parents. They .... (ask) me about my day.

8 I .... (sleep). I fell asleep while I .... (do) my homework!

3 🔊 2.1 Listen and check your answers.

4 What were you doing at these times yesterday? Write a sentence for each one.

1 `07:00 a.m.` ....
....

2 `10:00 a.m.` ....
....

3 `01:00 p.m.` ....
....

4 `05:00 p.m.` ....
....

5 `08:00 p.m.` ....
....

6 `10:00 p.m.` ....
....

5 Choose the correct words to complete the sentences.

1 While I **lived / was living** in Japan, I **took / was taking** Japanese lessons.

2 What **were they talking / did they talk** about when I **came / was coming** into the room?

3 Our host family **didn't speak / weren't speaking** to us in Spanish while we **stayed / were staying** with them.

4 When we **arrived / were arriving**, all the guests **danced / were dancing**.

5 I **didn't use / wasn't using** my phone while we **travelled / were travelling**.

6 She **spoke / was speaking** in a strange language, so I **wasn't / wasn't being** able to understand her.

6 Complete the conversation with the past simple or past continuous form of the verbs in brackets.

A: [1] .... (you / take) a lot of study books or a travel guide with you on your language exchange?

B: No, I [2] .... (not need) them. I just [3] .... (put) my smartphone in my pocket. When I [4] .... (study) and needed to look up a word, I [5] .... (use) an online dictionary. When I [6] .... (sightsee), my phone [7] .... (become) both a map and a guidebook. And of course it was also my camera.

A: I see! So you [8] .... (not have to) carry a heavy bag.

B: Exactly! My phone weighs next to nothing, so I [9] .... (not get) tired while I [10] .... (walk) around.

VOCABULARY

language and communication

1 Complete the crossword.

Across

3 say a word with the correct sounds
4 know what something means
6 tell someone about something so they can understand it
8 say things as part of a conversation
9 speak words
10 know that a sound is being made
12 say or do something again

Down

1 change words from one language to another language
2 have a definition or explanation
5 talk to people; say and understand words of a language
7 pay attention to what someone is saying or to a sound
11 give information to someone

2 🔊 2.2 Listen to six short conversations. When you hear the beep, decide which of these words is missing.

| explain | mean | pronounce | repeat | speak | understand |

1 .... 4 ....
2 .... 5 ....
3 .... 6 ....

3 🔊 2.3 Listen and check your answers.

4 Choose the correct words to complete the sentences.

1 Do you **tell / talk / say** to your friends about your problems?
2 I didn't know. Thank you for **talking / telling / saying** me.
3 Who were you **saying / telling / talking** to on the phone?
4 I'm sorry, I can't **hear / listen / speak** you because it's too noisy in here.
5 Sorry, what did you **tell / talk / say**?
6 Do you want to **listen / hear / tell** to music or watch a film?

5 Complete the blog post with these verbs.

explain   pronounce   repeat   say   speak   translate   understand

Chinese whispers

I'm so excited to finally be in Beijing! We're travelling in China for three months. I'm learning to
1 .... Chinese, but at the moment people often don't 2 .... what I 3 ....
to them. I use my hands a lot to help 4 ....
what I mean. I point at things and I 5 ....
everything several times. Finally,
I ask my Chinese friend to
6 .... for me.
The problem is that I don't
7 .... the words
correctly and I get the
intonation wrong. Chinese is
a very difficult language!

6 Complete the sentences to make them true for you.

1 I never listen to ....
2 I find it difficult to pronounce the word ....
3 A word or phrase that I say too often is ....
4 The person I talk to the most is ....
5 I don't really understand the word .... in English.

Extend

7 🔊 2.4 Listen to seven different situations. Match the speaker or conversation (1–7) with what they are doing (A–G).

A making a complaint   ....
B giving an explanation   ....
C giving a greeting   ....
D making an excuse   ....
E interrupting someone   ....
F making a comment   ....
G thinking out loud   ....

LISTENING

1 ◄» 2.5 Listen to a teacher telling her students about a computer course. Which of these things does she talk about?

1 the type of course

2 when the course will take place

3 the teachers' experience

4 the cost

5 face-to-face lessons

6 what the course includes

2 Read the sentences (1–4). What type of word (A–D) is needed to fill each gap?

1 The fee for the course is £........ .

2 We'll start at ....

3 Please bring ....

4 .... will teach the course.

A a person

B a thing

C a number

D a time

TechLang
computer course

Online

You can learn how to create ¹............................ .

You have video lessons and do ²............................ .

You pay ³£ .... for the course.

You must complete a course assignment to receive a ⁴............................ .

Face-to-face

You attend face-to-face lessons organised by ⁵............................ .

You need to bring a ⁶............................ with you if you're twelve or under.

3 ℯ ◄» 2.6 Listen again and complete the sentences in the advertisement. Write one or two words or a number or a date or a time.

-ing form

4 Complete the course review with the -ing form of these verbs.

| create | do | improve | know | learn | spend | watch | work |

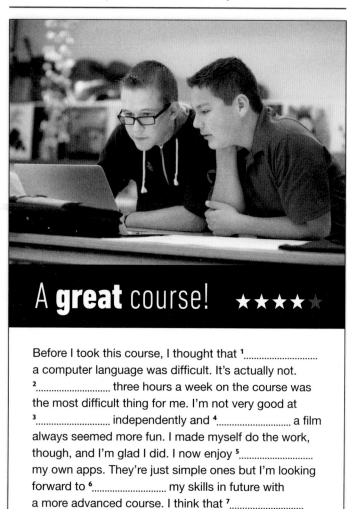

A **great** course! ★★★★☆

Before I took this course, I thought that ¹............................ a computer language was difficult. It's actually not. ²............................ three hours a week on the course was the most difficult thing for me. I'm not very good at ³............................ independently and ⁴............................ a film always seemed more fun. I made myself do the work, though, and I'm glad I did. I now enjoy ⁵............................ my own apps. They're just simple ones but I'm looking forward to ⁶............................ my skills in future with a more advanced course. I think that ⁷............................ a course like this is good for all teenagers. ⁸............................ how to program will probably be a really useful skill in the future.

5 Complete the sentences to make them true for you. Use the -ing form.

1 I love .... in the evenings.

2 I'm really good at ....

3 I'm pretty bad at ....

4 .... is my least favourite thing to do.

5 I don't like .... at the weekends.

6 .... is difficult for me.

7 .... is quite easy for me.

SPEAKING

1 Put the words in the correct order to make sentences describing different photos.

1 photo / a typical scene / shows / this / in a supermarket

....

....

2 two people / are / and a few others / in the background / in this photo, / there

....

....

3 that / was taken / I guess / in a supermarket / this photo

....

....

4 all the people / that's / look / because / very busy

....

....

5 definitely / for a bus / the couple / waiting / are

....

....

6 the man / and the woman / I'm / know each other / sure

....

....

2 Look at the photo of people talking in a town centre. Complete the sentences about the photo with one word in each gap.

1 One of the people is wearing a .... on their head.

2 In the foreground, there are some skateboards and two ....

3 Three of the teenagers are sitting on a ....

4 In the background, there are some blocks of .... or buildings.

5 The three people on the right are listening to the boy on the ....

6 I think that the photo wasn't taken inside. It was taken ....

7 There are .... people in the photo.

8 Two of the people have long hair. The other two have .... dark hair.

9 The boy on the right is sitting on the ....

10 The girl dressed in a white top has got a pair of .... around her neck.

3 🔊 2.7 Listen to the sentences from Ex 2 and check your answers. Is there anything else you could say about the photo?

4 Which words or phrases in Ex 2 help the speakers to describe the photo? Can you find any more in Ex 1?

5 Match the sentences in Ex 2 (1–10) with the functions (A–E).

A introducing the people: ....

B saying where the photo was taken: ....

C describing the place: .... , ...

D saying what the people look like or are wearing: .... , ... , ...

E saying what the people are doing: .... , ... , ...

6 Now look at the photo on page 10. Record yourself describing the photo. How many of the describing words and phrases from Exs 1 and 2 can you use?

WRITING

a story

1 Read the writing task and match the questions (1–5) with the notes (A–E).

> Your English teacher has asked you to write a story. Your story must begin with this sentence:
>
> ## We expected to have a great evening.
>
> Write your **story** in about **100 words**.

1 When did it happen? ....
2 Where did it happen? ....
3 Who was there? ....
4 What was the main action / situation / problem? ....
5 What happened in the end? ....

A a restaurant; good food, huge, not busy
B paid bill (expensive!); left feeling angry
C on holiday
D terrible food and service
E me and my family; a few other customers

2 Read a student's story. Replace the words in brackets with these words.

| delicious | disgusting | furious | hilarious | huge | terrible |

An evening to forget

We expected to have a great evening. We were on holiday. We decided to eat at a restaurant that described its food as ¹(very nice) .... It was ²(very big) .... but there weren't many people there. We soon found out why.

The waitress didn't remember what we asked for and brought us the wrong food. At first we thought it was ³(very funny) .... but when she brought us the wrong things a second time, we stopped laughing. It was late, so we decided to eat the food. Unfortunately, it was ⁴(not nice) .... Then things got worse when she dropped a drink on my dad – and the drink wasn't even for him!

After so many mistakes, they were ⁵(very angry) .... when they saw the bill. It was extremely expensive and no discount had been offered. We all agreed that going there was a ⁶(very bad) .... decision!

3 Think about a situation where you had an experience that wasn't what you expected. Make a list of strong adjectives that describe that event.

....
....
....

4 Read the task in Ex 1 again and choose a real or imaginary situation you would like to write about. Can you think of a second sentence for your story that could follow the first sentence given in the task?

1 When did it happen?
....

2 Where did it happen?
....

3 Who was there?
....

4 What was the main action / situation / problem?
....

5 What happened in the end?
....

5 ⊖ Write your story in about 100 words. Use your notes from Ex 3 to help you.

UNIT CHECK

1 Complete the sentences with the past simple or past continuous form of the verbs in brackets.

1 I .... (study) Turkish in Istanbul when I .... (meet) my friend Elif.

2 While we .... (swim), some friends .... (hide) our towels as a joke!

3 When I .... (get) home, my mum .... (talk) to someone on the phone.

4 Lucy .... (chat) to one of her teachers when I .... (see) her.

5 I .... (slip) and fell while I .... (run) down the stairs. So embarrassing!

6 My brothers and I .... (have) a huge fight while we .... (walk) to school yesterday.

7 The radio .... (be) on but I .... (not listen) to it.

8 While Matthew .... (look) down at his phone, he .... (walk) into a lamppost!

2 Write the questions to complete the conversations. Use the information in bold to help you.

1 A: ....
B: No, she didn't invite **Stephen** but she invited Alex.

2 A: ....
B: Six o'clock? We were doing **our homework**.

3 A: ....
B: I think he worked **in an Italian restaurant** last summer.

4 A: ....
B: They wanted **some help** with their maths.

5 A: ....
B: No, I wasn't **sleeping when he called**! I was checking my emails.

6 A: ....
B: I was talking to **my neighbour Sam** when you saw me.

7 A: ....
B: No, Jo, she wasn't **laughing at you**! She was watching a comedy!

8 A: ....
B: They were **at home** last night.

3 Find and correct the mistakes with *-ing* forms in four of the sentences.

1 Swim is really good for you.

....

2 Come on! We need to hurrying up!

....

3 I really enjoy getting out on my bike.

....

4 I can't study without listen to music.

....

5 I'm pretty good at make new friends.

....

4 Match 1–6 with A–F to make sentences.

1 I can't read the article aloud ....
2 They speak very quietly ....
3 It's difficult to translate poetry ....
4 I want to remember the words ....
5 They didn't understand the first time ....
6 It's difficult to explain on the phone ....

A so I'm explaining it again.
B because the sound is as important as the meaning.
C because you can't see the picture.
D because I don't know how to pronounce the words.
E so I'm repeating them many times.
F so it's hard to hear what they're saying.

5 Choose the correct words to complete the sentences.

1 Don't **say / tell** me the answer. I want to work it out for myself.
2 What language do they **talk / speak** in Egypt?
3 Do you **mean / say** you don't know or you don't want to tell me?
4 I **understand / translate** spoken Japanese, but find it difficult to read.
5 What did you **pronounce / say**?
6 Can you **repeat / tell** the words? I didn't hear the difference.
7 **Listen / Hear**! This is important information.
8 Let me **speak / explain** how to send a text message.

6 Complete the restaurant review with these words. You do not need three of the words.

---

accent   complaint   excuse   explanation   greeting
interrupted   out loud   repeated   translation

@Blogger15

My family and I were looking forward to eating at this restaurant but the menu was in the local language and we couldn't understand it. We asked the waiter for a menu with an English ¹........................... but he didn't have one. He tried to give us an ²........................... of each item on the menu but it was taking him ages and his ³........................... was hard for us to understand, so it didn't help. My dad ⁴........................... him and said we'd be OK. I tried to read some of the meals ⁵........................... to see if that helped but it didn't. In the end, we made an ⁶........................... about not feeling well and left.

3 The future is now

READING

1 Complete the words in the sentences. Use the meanings in brackets to help you.

1 He's a new artist but websites p _ _ _ _ t that he will be really famous. (say something will happen)

2 It's c _ _ _ _ n for young people to listen to new music. (happening often)

3 It's possible to p _ _ _ _ e music at home these days, using simple equipment. (make)

4 I'm going to see my first l _ _ e concert tomorrow. (not recorded)

5 After the concert, we went d _ _ _ _ _ _ y home. (without going somewhere else)

6 She's an i _ _ _ _ _ _ _ _ e performer! I never miss her shows! (so good I cannot believe it)

7 My brother sings and plays the guitar in the school b _ _ d. (a group of musicians)

8 Unfortunately, their first album wasn't very s _ _ _ _ _ _ _ l. (selling many copies)

2 Read the article quickly. What is the main idea? Choose the correct answer.

A how to get tickets to see a band

B choosing the right band to see

C tips for attending a concert

3 e Read the article again. Five sentences have been removed from the article. Complete the text with these sentences (A–H). There are three extra sentences which you do not need to use.

A Avoid sandals and wear trainers instead.

B It's not possible to do it all.

C If this isn't for you, move away.

D Take a spare battery if you have one.

E This can be both tiring and boring.

F You'll definitely want to try it out.

G This includes a pen for when you meet the band.

H Think about the essential things you'll need.

4 Read the article again. Are the following statements true (T) or false (F)?

The writer thinks:

1 going to a concert is better than watching a band on TV. ....

2 you should always arrive very early. ....

3 the most important thing is to look good. ....

4 you shouldn't take a bag. ....

5 it's important to take a phone or a camera. ....

6 it's easier to dance if you stand at the back. ....

5 Find words in the article that have these meanings.

1 a performance, concert, competition, etc. that many people watch or take part in (para 1) ....

2 some; more than a few (para 2) ....

3 put your foot on something (para 3) ....

4 things (para 4) ....

5 energy to make a machine work (para 5) ....

6 active and full of energy (para 6) ....

6 Complete the sentences with the words from Ex 5.

1 I've got so much .... in my bag, it's making my back hurt!

2 Please be careful not to .... the beautiful flowers.

3 Teachers know students are always more .... in the morning.

4 The .... is being organised to raise money for the new hospital.

5 I tried to call you .... times last night. Where were you?

6 It's surprising, but a hairdryer needs a lot of .... to work.

Seeing your favourite band LIVE

Going to my first concert was one of the most brilliant things I've ever done. Watching a band play live is so much better than watching a recording on TV. However, concerts have their problems, so here are some things you should think about before you go to your first live music event.

First, if there are no seats, plan with your friends or family where to stand before you go. If you want to be near the stage, you'll need to arrive very early. This means several hours on your feet before the band appears. [1]............................. I'd suggest you only do it for a band you really love.

What you wear is really important. Two things are sure: you're going to get hot and people will tread on your toes. This means you shouldn't wear anything too heavy except perhaps on your feet. [2]............................. You can look good and be comfortable at the same time.

Don't take too much stuff or you'll get bored carrying it around. [3]............................. These include your ticket, some money and your phone. You can put these into your pocket or a small bag. Make sure everything is safe during the concert.

You'll want to take a phone or camera to take lots of photos. Make sure it has enough power and memory for the whole evening. [4]............................. It'll help you take all the photos you want to remember the event.

Finally, remember that people will dance around during the concert. This means you'll probably get pushed. If it's a lively band, the audience might go a bit crazy. [5]............................. Stand near the back. You can still enjoy the concert from there. You'll have more space to dance too. Yes, dance. Above all, dance and have a great time!

3 The future is now

GRAMMAR

the future

1 Put the words in the correct order to make sentences.

1 he / pay / is / your ticket / to / for / going?

....

2 your / birthday / 'll / a cake / for / make / I

....

3 probably / we / late / be / 'll / dinner / tonight / for

....

4 concert / at / the / eight o'clock / starts

....

5 're / Jack / this evening / meeting / we

....

6 going / their album / not / I / buy / 'm / to

....

7 love / sure / 'm / his new song / I / 'll / you

....

8 starting / your / you / when / are / drum lessons?

....

2 Complete the sentences with the correct form of the verbs in brackets. Use *will* or the present continuous.

1 It's really hot in here. I .... (turn up) the air conditioning.

2 We can help you tidy up. We .... (put) the dirty plates in the dishwasher.

3 Harry wants to change his job, so he .... (meet) a careers advisor next week.

4 When we get a smart fridge, we .... (not waste) any food.

5 You've got your coat on. Where .... (you / go)?

6 I .... (do) any exercise tonight. I'm too tired.

7 Don't worry, I .... (explain) how this works.

8 We .... (have) a party tomorrow. Do you want to come?

3 Complete the conversation between two brothers with the correct form of the verbs in brackets. Use *will* or *going to*.

A: Where are you going, Tim?

B: To the computer shop. I **¹**........................... (buy) a new game.

A: I'm bored. I **²**........................... (come) with you.

B: OK. The game I want is quite new, so it **³**........................... (not take) long to find it.

B: Ah, here it is. There's no price on it. Excuse me, how much is this?

C: Let me check. This one's forty-five euros but we **⁴**........................... (have) a sale soon, so it **⁵**........................... (probably / be) cheaper then.

B: Thanks! I **⁶**........................... (not buy) it today, then.

A: I **⁷**........................... (meet) my friend in town next weekend. I can get it for you then if you like.

B: Oh that would be great – thanks, Jon!

4 🔊 3.1 Listen and check your answers.

5 Choose the correct verb forms to complete the email.

To: Katie

From: Max

Subject: Concert

Hi Katie,

What **¹are you doing / will you do** next Saturday? I **²go / 'm going to** see some local bands play in the park. Do you want to come with me? I've got a spare ticket. The concert **³is starting / starts** at eight and I guess it **⁴'s finishing / 'll finish** around 11 p.m. I **⁵'ll probably take / probably take** the bus to the park and I've already organised a lift home. My dad **⁶picks / 's picking** me up at 11 p.m. outside the sailing club.

I went to the same event last year and it was fun, so I'm sure it **⁷'s going to be / 's good** again this year. I expect there **⁸'ll be / is** food there too, so we can get something to eat before the main band comes on. Let me know what you think.

Max

6 Write a short paragraph about your plans for the weekend.

VOCABULARY

technology in the home

1 Match words (1–6) with words (A–F) to make compound nouns. Which two nouns are written as one word?

1	dish	**A**	wave
2	fridge-	**B**	machine
3	micro	**C**	freezer
4	remote	**D**	TV
5	smart	**E**	washer
6	washing	**F**	control

2 Look at the pictures and complete the sentences.

1 We can heat up yesterday's leftover pizza in the ....

2 My parents have a .... which makes an espresso in less than a minute.

3 Keeping vegetables in the .... helps them last longer.

4 Is that a .... ? Can you download apps onto it?

5 I need to turn the TV off. Where's the .... ?

6 Put the .... on and boil some water for a cup of tea, will you?

7 Harry, look at all these dirty clothes! Don't you know where the .... is?

8 All the plates and cups in the .... are clean. Can you put them away, please?

3 Choose the correct phrasal verbs to complete the sentences.

1 Remember to **switch off / turn down / go off** the lights when you go out.

2 Can you **turn up / turn down / switch on** the TV? It's too loud.

3 It's too dark in here. I'll **turn off / shut down / switch on** the light.

4 As soon as I've **gone off / set up / shut down** my new phone, I'll send you my number.

5 I need to **switch on / plug in / turn down** my phone. My battery's low.

6 Please **pick up / switch off / turn up** the heating. I'm cold.

7 **Switch on / Plug in / Shut down** the computer, will you? We don't need it on.

4 Complete the sentences to make them true for you.

1 I like to turn my music up loud when ....

2 I usually switch off the TV when ....

3 I usually charge up my phone when ....

4 I turn down the radio when ....

5 🔊 3.2 Listen to Charlotte telling her friend Grace about her holiday. What was the problem?

6 🔊 3.3 Complete the words in the sentences from the recording. The first letter of each word is given. Listen again and check your answers.

1 The power w.......................... o..........................
for two days!

2 We couldn't heat any food because the m.......................... wasn't working.

3 We ate cold stuff from the f.......................... .

4 We had to wash plates by hand in cold water because we couldn't use the d.......................... .

5 I couldn't p.......................... i..........................
my phone, so the battery died.

6 The wi-fi s.......................... o..........................
too, of course, so there was no internet.

Extend

7 Complete the phrasal verbs in the blog post with these prepositions.

back   down   out (x3)   up (x2)   with

What is the weather going to be like today?

Send a text message to David.

A DIGITAL assistant

All of our smartphones and tablets have a built-in digital assistant these days. You press a button, ask a question and the assistant finds **1** .... the answer for you. One day, our digital assistant will end **2** .... organising all aspects of our lives. She'll carry **3** .... boring chores for us, such as ordering the weekly shopping. She'll help us get **4** .... home if we're lost. If the car breaks **5** .... , she'll call a mechanic and ask them to come and fix it. In fact, any problem we have, our assistant will deal **6** .... it by calling someone who can help. We might even find that our assistant is happy to call up our partner and break **7** .... with them for us! I'm not sure that's true, but the biggest problem will be how dependent we are on the assistant. We won't know what to do when our phone runs **8** .... of battery!

Add pasta to my shopping list.

LISTENING

1 Read the questions (1–7) in Ex 3 and match them with the purpose of each conversation (A–G).

A talking about different game genres ....

B choosing useful materials for studying ....

C talking about something which isn't working ....

D discussing what to get when shopping ....

E finding out when a business opens ....

F talking about their interest in a concert ....

G talking about online material they enjoy using ....

2 Read the questions in Ex 3 again and look at the pictures. What words do you think you will hear in each conversation? Match the questions (1–7) to the words below.

blog	5	magic	
dictionary		microwave	
dishwasher		morning	
DJ		quarter to nine	
girl band		racing	
hand in		song	
keyboard		speakers	

3 🄴 🔊 3.4 Listen to the conversations. For each question, choose the correct answer.

1 What will the girl buy from the shop?

Ⓐ Ⓑ Ⓒ

2 What will the boy use to do his homework?

Ⓐ Ⓑ Ⓒ

3 Which type of game is the girl's favourite?

Ⓐ Ⓑ Ⓒ

4 Who does the boy want to see in concert?

Ⓐ  Ⓑ  Ⓒ

5 What website does the girl use most often?

Ⓐ  Ⓑ  Ⓒ

6 Which machine has broken down?

Ⓐ  Ⓑ  Ⓒ

7 What time will the mobile phone shop open?

Ⓐ Ⓑ Ⓒ

advice and suggestions

4 Choose the correct words to complete the conversation.

A: ¹**How / Why** don't we watch a film later?

B: Good idea. We ²**ought / should** watch the latest Marvel film. I think Ben has the DVD.

A: We ³**could / might** download it – it's probably easier.

B: OK, good idea. ⁴**Shall / Will** I do that now?

A: Yes. Then we can watch it when we want to. And we ⁵**could / ought** to get some popcorn. I'll go to the shop.

B: Great! How about ⁶**get / getting** some of that sweet and salty popcorn? I love that!

A: Sounds good. I'll see what they've got.

5 🔊 3.5 Listen and check your answers.

6 Your teacher has asked for suggestions for an end-of-year class event. Complete the sentences to make some suggestions.

1 How about .... ?

2 Why don't we .... ?

3 We should ....

4 We could ....

5 We ought to ....

SPEAKING

1 🔊 3.6 Listen to sentences about about different ways of watching films. Complete the sentences with the words the speakers use.

agree   for   point   right   sure   think   true   view

1 I .... a tablet's useful. If you download a film onto it, you can watch it anywhere.

2 That's .... And the screen's bigger than a mobile.

3 Yes, that's a good .... Maybe a tablet's useful for watching a film at home, then.

4 You're .... I'd like a room like that. It's better to watch a film with other people.

5 Hmm, I'm not .... I prefer to watch films alone.

6 .... me , laptops are great for video clips, but they aren't so good for films.

7 I don't ....

8 In my .... , it's more fun to watch films with other people.

2 🔊 3.7 Listen again. Look at the pictures (A–E) and decide which of these things the speakers agree on?

3 Match the highlighted phrases in Ex 1 to the correct column in the table.

giving opinions	agreeing	disagreeing

4 Complete the conversation with phrases from the table in Ex 3.

A: I don't like any of these films. **1**.......................... they're boring.

B: Really? **2**.......................... . I think they're all really interesting.

A: They're all action films. What's interesting about that?

B: Well, yes, **3**.......................... – they *are* action films. But they have good stories too. I mean, there are some deeper messages in them.

A: **4**.......................... about that. They don't seem very deep to me. **5**.......................... , action films focus too much on special effects and not enough on the story.

B: Yes, **6**.......................... , but only for some action films. You have to choose the right ones to watch.

5 🔊 3.8 Listen to the questions and record your answers. Listen to your answers. How many of the phrases from Ex 3 did you use?

WRITING

an email

1 Read the writing task and the email and notes below. Then read statements 1–4 and decide if they are true (T) or false (F).

Read this email from an English-speaking friend and the notes you have made. Write your email using all the notes. Write your answer in about 100 words.

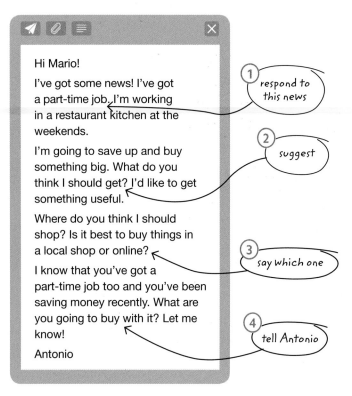

Hi Mario!

I've got some news! I've got a part-time job. I'm working in a restaurant kitchen at the weekends.

I'm going to save up and buy something big. What do you think I should get? I'd like to get something useful.

Where do you think I should shop? Is it best to buy things in a local shop or online?

I know that you've got a part-time job too and you've been saving money recently. What are you going to buy with it? Let me know!

Antonio

1 — respond to this news
2 — suggest
3 — say which one
4 — tell Antonio

1 Antonio has written you a letter. ....
2 He has some good news. ....
3 He is writing to arrange a meeting with you. ....
4 You have to respond to four different things in the email. ....
5 You must write more than 100 words. ....

2 Match the ideas (A–G) with the notes in Ex 1 (1–4).

A better customer service in shop ....
B new phone — you can do lots of things on it ....
C electric guitar — I want to start a band! ....
D congratulations ....
E can ask more questions ....
F your phone is old! ....
G I want to make my own music ....

3 Match 1–7 with A–G to make sentences giving advice and making suggestions.

1 You ought   A getting a set of speakers for your phone?
2 How about   B you get a new laptop?
3 You could   C some really good headphones.
4 Why don't   D get a tablet.
5 You should get   E I send you the website address?
6 Shall   F idea to get it online.
7 It's a good   G to get a more up-to-date phone.

4 Complete Mario's email with one word in each gap.

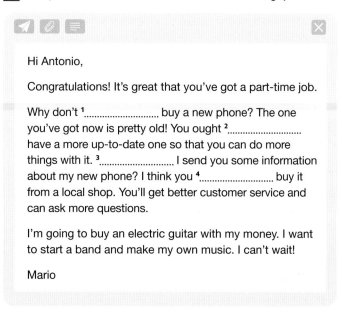

Hi Antonio,

Congratulations! It's great that you've got a part-time job.

Why don't ¹........................... buy a new phone? The one you've got now is pretty old! You ought ²........................... have a more up-to-date one so that you can do more things with it. ³........................... I send you some information about my new phone? I think you ⁴........................... buy it from a local shop. You'll get better customer service and can ask more questions.

I'm going to buy an electric guitar with my money. I want to start a band and make my own music. I can't wait!

Mario

5 Read Mario's email again. Does he include all four points in the exam task in Ex 1? Are the ideas organised clearly?

6 **e** Read the writing task again and write your own email in about 100 words. Try to use different phrases for giving advice and making suggestions.

UNIT CHECK

1 Choose the correct words to complete the conversation.

A: What ¹**are you doing / will you do** at the weekend?

B: ²**I'm meeting / I'll meet** my friend Ella in town on Saturday to go shopping.

A: ³**Are you going to / Will you** buy anything?

B: Yes, ⁴**I get / I'm going to get** a birthday present for my sister.

A: Sounds great! ⁵**I'm going to / I'll** come with you, if that's OK.

B: OK, great! ⁶**I'm not going to / I won't** take a lot of money because I don't want to spend too much.

A: Yeah, I probably ⁷**am not going to / won't** spend a lot of money either.

B: OK, let's get the bus together. ⁸**I pay / I'll pay** for your ticket. I owe you money from last week.

2 Match the sentences (1–6) with their functions (A–F). Look at the future forms in bold to help you.

1 **I'm seeing** the doctor at four this afternoon. ....
2 I don't think the teacher **will give** us homework tonight. ....
3 Jack and I **are going to have** a snowball fight. ....
4 You**'re not going to sleep** after seeing that scary film! ....
5 The programme **starts** at 9. ....
6 **I'll carry** those books for you. ....

A an arrangement
B a timetabled event
C an offer
D a prediction based on opinion
E a prediction based on outside knowledge
F a future plan or intention

3 Read the clues and complete the crossword with words for technology in the home.

Across

6 You use this to change channels on the TV. (2 words)
7 You clean plates in this.

Down

1 You make a cup of coffee with this. (2 words)
2 You clean clothes in this. (2 words)
3 You heat food in this.
4 You can stream TV programmes on this using wifi. (2 words)
5 You boil water in this.

4 Complete the phrasal verbs in the sentences. The first letter of each verb is given.

1 My phone's almost out of battery. I need to p............................ it in.
2 Shall I s............................ down your laptop or do you need to use it?
3 Can you please t............................ that music down? It's just too loud!
4 I'll help you s............................ up your new speakers. I want to hear how they sound.
5 Don't forget to s............................ off the lights when you leave the room.
6 Our electricity often g............................ off during a storm. It's always a bit scary!

5 Complete the conversation with one word in each gap.

A: So, we need to prepare a video presentation for our English homework. What do you think we ¹............................ talk about?

B: How ²............................ our favourite website?

A: Hmm, I think someone else is doing that. ³............................ don't we talk about the best places to visit in our town?

B: That's a good idea. And maybe we ⁴............................ film ourselves in those different places, talking about them.

A: Brilliant! ⁵............................ about doing that on Saturday?

B: Sure. I'm free then. But we ought ⁶............................ check it's OK with our parents first.

REVIEW: UNITS 1–3

1 Complete the blog post with the correct form of the verbs in brackets.

> I usually ¹............................ (work) Saturday and Sunday mornings in a bakery, but this week I ²............................ (work) extra hours because I ³............................ (save) for a new tablet. So my new routine is I ⁴............................ (get up) at 4.30 a.m., I ⁵............................ (go) to work, then I ⁶............................ (cycle) to school. After school I ⁷............................ (do) my homework and finally I ⁸............................ (go) to sleep. I ⁹............................ (enjoy) it because I know I ¹⁰............................ (make) lots of money but I ¹¹............................ (also / get) very tired!

2 Read what four young people are saying about their likes and dislikes. Complete the texts with these words.

about   at (x3)   in   of   on   with (x2)

Jana

> I'm frightened ¹............................ speaking in public and I don't like parties because I'm not good ²............................ talking to people I don't know. I prefer to hang out with my close friends.

> I love playing tennis and football. I get excited ³............................ competitions. I don't understand how people can sit still. I always want to run and dance. I love parties, I play the saxophone and I get fed up ⁴............................ people telling me to be quiet!

Evie

Charlie

> I work hard and get good grades. I'm interested ⁵............................ learning new things and quick to understand new information. My teacher also says that I'm brilliant ⁶............................ organising people and explaining things to them.

> I love making people laugh and I'm good ⁷............................ telling jokes. I'm also very keen ⁸............................ telling stories, but my friends don't like them as much as my jokes. They say they sometimes get bored ⁹............................ my stories.

Daniel

3 Read the texts in Ex 2 again. Complete the sentences with personality adjectives. Some letters are given.

1 Jana is s_ _ . She isn't c_ _ _ _ _ _ _t.
2 Evie is s_o_ _y and no_ _y.
3 Charlie is b_s_ _ and c_ _v_ _ .
4 Daniel is f_ _ _y.

4 Make sentences in the past simple. Put the time expression in brackets in the correct place.

1 we / have / a holiday / when I / be / a child (every year)
2 we / our / spend / holidays / at the beach (often)
3 I / go / swimming (most days)
4 my parents / buy / me / an ice cream (usually)
5 my sister and I / find / interesting sea creatures on the beach (now and then)
6 we / take / them home (never)
7 we / be / happy to go to the beach (always)

5 Choose the correct words to complete the sentences.

1 Please **hear / listen to** what I'm **saying / talking**.
2 Can you **explain / translate** what you **understand / mean**?
3 What did they **tell / speak** you?
4 How do you **pronounce / repeat** this word? I don't know how to **speak / say** it.
5 I don't **explain / understand** what you're **talking / telling** about.
6 Can you **speak / translate** this word? I don't know what it **means / pronounces**.
7 Can you **repeat / talk** that, please? I didn't **listen to / hear** you.
8 I enjoy **listening to / hearing** my grandfather **talking / telling** stories.

6 Choose the most appropriate future forms to complete the text.

My brother, my sister and I have a plan. **¹We're all going to learn / We'll all learn** new skills this year.

Oliver **²learns / is going to learn** to play the drums. He says **³he's working / he'll work** very hard. His lessons **⁴begin / are going to begin** on Wednesday.

Sophie wants to learn to dance. Her friend from Hawaii **⁵is teaching / is going to teach** her hula dancing. **⁶They meet / They're meeting** for their first lesson at the weekend. **⁷They'll probably spend / They're probably spending** the whole day dancing!

⁸I'm going to study / I study Japanese. I know that **⁹I'll find / I'm finding** it hard to learn because I'm not very good at languages. I also know that learning Japanese **¹⁰isn't being / won't be** easy because the alphabet is so different. It will take a long time, but I've promised myself that **¹¹I'm not giving up / I won't give up**!

7 Complete the crossword.

Across

5 I've put the food in the f............................ –freezer to keep it fresh for tomorrow.

8 I'll heat your dinner in the m............................ .

10 I need a cup of tea. Can you put the k............................ on?

Down

1 I need to p............................ in my phone. The battery's nearly dead.

2 I've set my alarm to go o............................ at six tomorrow morning.

3 Please put the dirty plates in the d............................ .

4 All your dirty clothes are in the washing m............................ .

6 Can you t............................ down the heating? It's too hot in here.

7 Have you seen the r............................ control for the TV anywhere?

9 Do you want me to help you s............................ up your new laptop?

8 Complete the conversations with these words and phrases.

| could   how about   ought   shall I |
| shall we   should   why don't you |

1 A: What .... do with all these old clothes we have?

B: We .... give them a charity shop. That's one idea.

2 A: I can't see any belts in here.

B: We .... to try the shop across the road. They'll have them there.

3 A: We walk the same route home from school every day.

B: Well, ... taking a different route tomorrow?

4 A: I'm really stressed about my exams next week.

B: .... watch a film or something to relax?

5 A: I've made a terrible mess of this kitchen.

B: You .... clean it up before your parents get home!

6 A: I've got a horrible headache.

B: .... get you some tablets?

9  Read the article. For each question, choose the correct answer.

Saving **memory**

According to research, we're no longer **1**........ at remembering important information. Our friends' phone numbers, the way to the doctor's or the date of an aunt's birthday are all examples of this. However, there's a good reason why we don't remember this stuff. Why should we waste time learning something when we can simply **2**........ on our phones and look the information up?

Of course, looking up something we're **3**........ in online is a fast way to get information. Using the internet to **4**........ a foreign word into our own language is easy too. However, speed means that we probably won't be able to **5**........ the information or word to someone else twenty-four hours later. To get the word into our long-term memories, we have to think about what it **6**........ more deeply so that it sticks in our minds better.

1 A good	**B** able	**C** hard	**D** pleasant
2 A plug	**B** set	**C** carry	**D** switch
3 A keen	**B** interested	**C** excited	**D** amazed
4 A pronounce	**B** say	**C** understand	**D** translate
5 A explain	**B** argue	**C** talk	**D** speak
6 A intends	**B** means	**C** suggests	**D** identifies

Taking part

READING

1 Choose the correct words to complete the email.

Hi Beth,

I did it! I've never felt so tired in my life, but I did it! Can you believe I **¹kept / stood** going until the end of the race? All forty-two kilometres! When I crossed the finish line, it felt like I was running **²on / off** air! Thank you for making me **³make / take** my training seriously. The race was really tough, but I'm so glad I took **⁴place / part**!

Do you want to do a marathon with me next year? The New York marathon takes **⁵place / part** in the autumn. What do you think?

Love,
Emma

2 Read about five people (1–5) who want to join a swimming club. Answer the questions.

Who:

1 would like to take part in competitions? ....
2 is also skilled at a different sport? ....
3 prefers to be in a club with fewer people? ....
4 is bored with swimming in a pool? ....
5 wants to socialise with the other members of the club? ....
6 is busy every weekday? ....
7 wants to train with a teacher? ....
8 doesn't want something too easy? ....

3 **e** Read the advertisements for eight swimming clubs. Decide which club (A–H) would be the most suitable for the people (1–5).

1 Ava ....
2 Matthew ....
3 Alfie ....
4 Charlotte ....
5 Leigh ....

Ava is fourteen. She started swimming lessons when she was very young and isn't interested in going to swimming pools any more. She finds swimming outdoors very exciting. She isn't free on weekdays.

Matthew can swim well and is interested in learning how to race. He would like to have some sessions with an instructor. He is busy on Mondays and Wednesdays.

Alfie is sixteen. He enjoys swimming in his free time and is keen to meet other people who share the same hobby. He'd like to have fun after swimming, as well as in the pool.

Charlotte is thirteen. She knows how to swim but wants to feel more confident in the water. She'd like to join a small club and meet young people with the same level of ability. She'd prefer to do something during the week.

Leigh is an excellent gymnast as well as a very good swimmer. She would like to join a club where she is challenged to learn new things. She isn't free at the weekends.

Fun Swim: **find your club!**

A Town Swimming Club

This is a serious club for swimmers who are interested in representing our town in competitions. You don't need to be an expert to join us, as we provide training from qualified swimming instructors. There is a test to check your level before you start. We meet every Saturday. Ask the receptionist for an up-to-date timetable.

B Water Polo Club

If you love swimming and competitions, then our club is for you! We need new members to join our teams. There are two levels: beginners and intermediate. We provide extra equipment but you do need to wear a hat and goggles. We meet every Wednesday, 4.00 p.m. to 6.00 p.m.

C Swim For You

We are a friendly swimming club which meets on Friday evenings, from 5.00 p.m. onwards.

Each meeting starts with an hour-long swimming session at the Heath Road pool and then there is a chance for our members to get to know each other, with refreshments provided. Open to young people aged fifteen and above.

D Wild-Swimming

Do you enjoy swimming in the open air? Then put on your wetsuit and come wild-swimming with us! We meet on Sundays at the Heath Road pool and take a minibus to the lake. Instructors will be available to help you make the most of your time and stay safe. You must be an excellent swimmer to join.

E Improve Your Swimming

If you are not a beginner swimmer but would like to improve your technique, this is the club for you. Numbers are limited, so our members can get attention from an instructor whenever they want. Our club meets on Tuesdays from 4.30 p.m. to 5.30 p.m.

F Dolphins Swimming Club

We are a club for kids who love to swim! Each week we try a new sport or game and afterwards there is time for a snack and a chat in the main hall. The club is open to anyone aged 10–14 who can already swim 25 metres without help. We meet on Saturday afternoons at 3 p.m.

G Aqua Club

What could be more fun than keeping fit in the water? Aqua aerobics is like doing gymnastics underwater. It's great for building muscles and keeping in shape. The club meets every Saturday and there are two levels: 10.00 a.m. for beginners and 11.00 a.m. for swimmers who have tried aqua aerobics before.

H Synchro-Swim

We're looking for new members for the synchronised swimming club. Do you think you've got what it takes to join us? You need to be a confident swimmer with dance or gymnastics training to start learning this fantastic sport. Previous members of our club have been selected for the national team. Sessions are on Mondays from 5.00 p.m. to 6.30 p.m.

4 Find words or phrases in the article that have these meanings.

1 with all the latest information (text A) ....
2 lesson (text C) ....
3 food and drink (text C) ....
4 outside (text D) ....
5 fit (text G) ....
6 chosen (text H) ....

5 Complete the sentences with words or phrases from Ex 4.

1 Is this the most .... version of the members list? It looks quite old.
2 Running is good for your heart and for staying ....
3 Take sandwiches and some juice because there aren't any .... at the sports centre.
4 I've .... the players for the volleyball team. They're on that list on the wall.
5 I love exercising ...., especially on warm days.
6 Our next training .... is on Monday afternoon.

GRAMMAR

present perfect

1 Choose the correct verb forms to complete the sentences.

1 **I'm / I've** never tried climbing, but I'd like to.
2 I've **did / done** gymnastics since I was five years old.
3 **Has / Have** you or your friend ever been in a basketball team?
4 I've always **rode / ridden** a mountain bike, not a BMX.
5 We've just **finished / finishing** the game. I lost!

2 🔊 4.1 Listen to two teachers talking about preparations for sports day at their school. Which things has the woman already done?

School sports day — things to do

1 *wash team vests* ☐
2 *buy winners' medals* ☐
3 *write team lists* ☐
4 *find sacks for jumping race* ☐
5 *send email to parents* ☐
6 *check sound system* ☐
7 *ask Mr Granger to cut the grass* ☐

3 🔊 4.2 Complete the sentences from the recording with the present perfect form of the verbs in brackets. Listen again and check your answers.

1 .... (you / ever / help) with sports day at school before?
2 I .... (already / tick) some things off the list, but you can help with the rest.
3 I .... (not buy) the medals yet.
4 Mrs Brown .... (already / look) in the sports storeroom.
5 .... (you / send) an email to the parents about sports day yet?
6 I .... (just / do) that. The sound system is fine.
7 Mr Granger .... (not cut) the grass yet.
8 .... (I / forget) anything?

4 Complete the sentences with these adverbs and the present perfect form of the verbs in brackets.

always   ever   just   never   yet

1 I .... (swim) in a lake in my life, but I'd like to.
2 They started training at 10.30 and they .... (not finish).
3 .... (you / see) a live sporting event?
4 I .... (love) team sports. They're fun!
5 Tom's hair is wet because he .... (have) a swimming lesson.

5 Choose which words or phrases go in which column in the table.

2016   a couple of hours   a few days   a month   last week   September   three years   we were little

for	since

6 Complete the blog post with the present perfect form of the verbs in brackets.

Our new sports centre

There are lots of new sports to try at the sports centre. It [1]... (just / open), so I couldn't wait to go and find out what's on offer. In fact, I [2]... (already / sign up) for two new sports!

I love swimming, and I'm quite good at it, but I [3]... (never / be) in a team before – I [4]... (always / swim) on my own. Now I [5]... (join) the new water polo team, which is very exciting. I [6]... (not meet) my teammates yet, though, because sessions start next week.

I'm also interested to learn about the sprint cycling because I [7]... (never / try) it before. I'm going to do a 'starter' ride on Saturday because I [8]... (not decide) if I want to join the group yet.

VOCABULARY

sport

1 Complete the conversation with these words.

changing rooms   coach   locker   prize   race   track

A: Excuse me, are these the girls' **1**.......................... ?

B: Yes, that's right. Come in. Do you want to put your bag in a **2**.......................... ?

A: Yes. The **3**.......................... told me to leave my things here.

B: You must be new. You'll like it here. We're preparing for an important cross-country **4**.......................... at the moment. It's called 'Five OK'!

A: Does that mean we have to go into the countryside to run?

B: No, we practise on the **5**.......................... first. We do shorter distances and practise starts and finishes.

A: And what's the **6**.......................... for winning 'Five OK'?

B: A silver cup, just like those ones over there. It's lovely!

2 Match the verbs (1–8) with A–H to make collocations.

1 lose ....
2 beat ....
3 win ....
4 score ....
5 train ....
6 hit ....
7 kick ....
8 compete ....

A against another team
B a tennis ball
C a football
D a match
E a goal
F an opponent
G for a competition
H a prize

3 **e** Choose the correct answers to complete the email.

Hi Mum,

I'm really enjoying summer camp. You won't believe it, but I'm in the top tennis group! We play **1**....... in pairs and groups of four. The tennis **2**....... are beautiful – and very big! We also **3**....... by hitting the ball against the wall. It sounds boring, but we have fun by seeing who can hit the most balls without stopping. Our **4**....... says it's a good way to train. He makes us work really hard – I guess that's why our group is the best! We play the groups from the other camps and we usually **5**....... them. But I think it's more fun to **6**....... against my friends than people I don't know.

One more week to enjoy and then back to school!

Love,
Kerry

1 A prizes	**B** matches	**C** goals	**D** races
2 A courts	**B** rooms	**C** tracks	**D** coaches
3 A kick	**B** coach	**C** score	**D** train
4 A player	**B** coach	**C** match	**D** team
5 A hit	**B** score	**C** beat	**D** win
6 A kick	**B** beat	**C** catch	**D** compete

Extend

4 Match these words with their meanings.

athlete   captain   champion   fan
final   medal   stadium

1 a prize which you can put around your neck ....

2 a person who competes in a sport ....

3 the last match in a competition ....

4 a place where thousands of people can watch live sport ....

5 a person who leads a team ....

6 someone who is very keen on a team or sportsperson ....

7 a person or team that wins a competition ....

5 🔊 4.3 Listen to an interview with a young man who loves football. Complete the notes with one word in each gap.

Name of super-**1**.........................:
Tom Lewis

Favourite place to watch football:
city **2**..........................

Favourite footballer: **3**.......................... of
the team, Wesley Richards

Reason: thinks Wesley is a great
4 ....

Favourite football moment: watching
the cup **5**.......................... at Wembley

Best football souvenir: **6**..........................
from the World Cup in Argentina

4 Taking part

LISTENING

1 🔊 **4.4 Listen to an interview with a young athlete who is talking about gymnastics. Which of these things does he talk about?**

1 what he finds difficult ☐
2 the time he spends training ☐
3 how gymnastics is affecting his school work ☐
4 what made him start training ☐
5 how gymnastics has changed him ☐
6 another sport he'd like to try ☐

2 🔊 **4.5 Listen again. For each question, choose the correct answer.**

1 How does Ryan feel about training at the gym?
 A He doesn't like having to work so hard.
 B He usually enjoys it even though it's not easy.
 C He'd prefer to stay in bed on weekdays.

2 What does Ryan find the most difficult about being a gymnast?
 A getting up early in the morning
 B eating a special diet
 C training under pressure

3 Ryan started gymnastics because
 A he saw a programme on television.
 B his mother made him do it.
 C his sister was a competitive gymnast.

4 What does Ryan say is his main motivation?
 A winning
 B becoming famous
 C being as good as other athletes

5 Ryan says that the key to being a successful athlete is
 A the time you put in.
 B having a good coach.
 C following certain rules.

6 Ryan feels that gymnastics has taught him
 A to be more confident.
 B to appreciate his family.
 C to organise his time.

past simple and present perfect

3 Choose the correct verb forms to complete the sentences.

1 Yesterday's match **was / has been** very exciting.
2 I **didn't run / haven't run** in the race this afternoon.
3 I **cycled / have cycled** to school today.
4 **Did the race finish / Has the race finished**? Who won?
5 **I knew / I've known** Ben for three years – we always play football together.
6 We **didn't play / haven't played** tennis since March!
7 The coach is late, so our training session **didn't start / hasn't started** yet.
8 When I was younger, I **didn't like / haven't liked** taking part in competitions.

4 Complete the email with the past simple or present perfect form of the verbs in brackets.

Hi Ethan,

Guess what! Our school ¹............................ (enter) the national sports competition and I ²............................ (decide) to take part! This year there are some new sports like synchronised swimming and mud running, which is great fun! The competition ³............................ (not include) these sports last year or the year before, so they're new for everyone. I ⁴............................ (not know) which sport to do until last week, when my teacher ⁵............................ (suggest) synchronised swimming. Of course, I ⁶............................ (say) 'yes'! I ⁷............................ (always / like) swimming, but I ⁸............................ (never / do) gymnastics in the water. It sounds fun – I can't wait!

Love,
Olivia

36

SPEAKING

1 Complete the questions about photo A with *what*, *where*, *who* or *how*.

1 .... is in the picture?
2 .... are they?
3 .... are they wearing?
4 .... are they doing?
5 .... are they feeling?
6 .... do you think about this sport?

2 Read a description of photo A. Does the student answer all the questions in Ex 1?

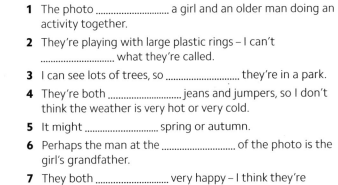
(A)

> The photo shows two friends. They are at the top of a rock and there are lots of trees around. They are wearing sports clothes, and one of them is also wearing a special hat. He is pulling a rope, so maybe he is helping a friend to climb up. I think it looks beautiful there, but a bit scary. I'd like to go climbing one day.

3 🔊 4.6 Listen to a student describing the same photo. Does he answer all the questions in Ex 1?

4 🔊 4.7 Listen again and decide the phrases you hear.

1 It's a photo of … ☐
2 On the left … ☐
3 On the right … ☐
4 At the back … ☐
5 At the front … ☐

6 It looks like … ☐
7 The boys look … ☐
8 I can't remember what it's called. ☐
9 It might be … ☐
10 Perhaps there's … ☐

5 Look at photo B. Complete the sentences describing it with one word in each gap. Use Exs 2 and 4 to help you.

1 The photo .... a girl and an older man doing an activity together.
2 They're playing with large plastic rings – I can't .... what they're called.
3 I can see lots of trees, so .... they're in a park.
4 They're both .... jeans and jumpers, so I don't think the weather is very hot or very cold.
5 It might .... spring or autumn.
6 Perhaps the man at the .... of the photo is the girl's grandfather.
7 They both .... very happy – I think they're having a great time.

6 Say the sentences in Ex 5. Record yourself.

7 🔊 4.8 Listen to your recording from Ex 6. Then listen to track 4.8. Compare.

(B)

WRITING

an article

1 Do you do any of these sports? Write your sports in the correct column in the table. Do you do any other activities that you can add?

basketball   cycling   football   rugby   running   table tennis   tennis   volleyball

at school	with my family	with my friends	I don't do these sports

2 Read the advert for an article about sports. How many questions do you need to answer? Highlight them.

Tell us about sport in your life!

We need a star article for the next edition of the school magazine. And it's all about sport.

- Which sports or games do you do or play and why?
- How good are you at those sports or games?
- How can sports or games help you in your life?

Tell us all about it — you might make the front page!

3 Complete a student's article with these words.

although   as soon as   because   either … or   except   so that

Sport and me

by Anna Richards

When I started school, I hated P.E. lessons because I didn't like team sports. I sometimes tried to hide in the library ¹ .... I didn't have to take part. Then, one day, one of my teachers said I should try throwing the javelin ² .... it isn't a team sport. And ³ .... I started, I loved it! I soon tried other athletic events too, like high jump and sprinting, and I liked most of them. Now I train most days, ⁴ .... before .... after school.

I'm good at most athletic events ⁵ .... long jump. My favourite is still the javelin. I represented my school in the national athletics championships last month. We won!

I'm much more confident now, and I find making new friends easier, ⁶ .... I still don't like team sports. Throwing the javelin also helps me to be strong and, of course, it keeps me fit.

4 Read the article in Ex 3 again and answer the questions.

1 Does the student answer all the questions in the advert?

....

2 Does she give extra information for each of the questions?

....

3 How many paragraphs are there? Which question does each paragraph answer?

....

....

4 Does the student use words and phrases to link ideas? Find examples.

....

....

5 Read the advert in Ex 2 again, then look at your answers to Ex 4 and plan your own article. Make notes for each paragraph.

....
....
....
....
....
....
....

6 **e** Write your article in about 100 words. Use your notes from Ex 5.

UNIT CHECK

1 Make sentences in the present perfect.

1 I / play / in a lot of football games this term

....

2 our team / not win / any matches this year

....

3 I not try / mud running, but I'd like to

....

4 you / put / your clothes in your locker?

....

5 Jacob / start / learning kickboxing with the new coach

....

6 the school / buy / some new footballs

....

2 Use the information in the table to write a paragraph about Jack and Amelia. Use the present perfect and *already* or *yet*.

	Jack	Amelia
buy tennis rackets	✓	✓
join a tennis club	✗	✗
have a tennis lesson	✗	✓
play a match	✗	✓

Jack and Amelia have decided to get fit. They have already

....

....

....

....

....

3 Complete the conversation with the present perfect or past simple form of the verbs in brackets.

A: Hey, you two. Look at all the new sports we can do at the sports centre.

B: ¹.............................. (you / try) sprint cycling?

A: No, I haven't got a bike. What about you?

B: I ².............................. (try) it last week but I ³.............................. (not like) it.

A: What about you, Dan?

C: I don't like sprint cycling either. I ⁴.............................. (join) the water polo team! We ⁵.............................. (have) a training session yesterday but we ⁶.............................. (not play) a match yet.

B: Maybe we should join, too.

A: I ⁷.............................. (never / play) water polo.

C: Well, why don't you come to the training session that's on this afternoon?

B: I can't. I ⁸.............................. (not finish) last week's homework yet.

A: I haven't got any homework. I'll come!

4 Label the pictures. The first letter of each word is given.

p..........................   m..........................

t.................. c..................   l..........................

t..................   c.................. r..........................

5 Complete the blog post with these verbs.

beat   competed   hit   kicked   scored   trained   won

Match report – Saturday 23 May

Today was a very important day because we ¹.......................... in our last match of the season. We've ².......................... for this for a long time. We needed to ³.......................... Greenfields High School to get to the top of the league.

No one ⁴.......................... in the first forty-five minutes – at half-time it was 0–0. As soon as we came out after the break, Harry ⁵.......................... the ball over the goalkeeper, but it ⁶.......................... the post and didn't go into the net.

Everyone was worried that it was too late, except me – I always believe in the team! And sure enough, with just five minutes to go, Rob got a goal and we ⁷.......................... ! We're in the number one spot for the first time! I'm signing off now to go and celebrate with the rest of the team.

5 In the spotlight

READING

1 Complete the sentences with these words.

attention   backs   due   right   stress   thing

1 No one has the .... to judge you because of how you look!

2 I've got exams soon, so I'm under a lot of .... at the moment.

3 The bus is late? That's the last .... I need!

4 His bad behaviour gets him negative .... from the teacher.

5 It's sad that her old friends have turned their .... on her now she's famous.

6 The delay in filming was .... to a problem with the cameras.

2 Read the article quickly and find:

1 the name of a fairytale character: ....

2 a place where two film stars got married: ....

3 two things photographers may use to get photos from above: ....

3 **e** Read the article again. For each question, choose the correct answer.

1 In the writer's opinion, we are interested in the weddings of celebrities because

 A we want to see their faces on their wedding day.

 B they are like friends to us.

 C we want to know what their lives are like.

 D they are our heroes.

2 What does the writer say about celebrities in the second paragraph?

 A Their weddings are private events.

 B They can't look perfect all the time.

 C Their lives are more exciting than ours.

 D They are just people like us.

3 The writer mentions Fassbender's wedding as an example of how some stars

 A keep their relationships private.

 B prefer to get married in another country.

 C get more attention from photographers.

 D try to avoid the public.

4 In Yolanda Burton's opinion, how can celebrity couples keep photographers away from their wedding?

 A by doing a deal with one publisher

 B by using technology

 C by posting free photographs online

 D by hiding

5 What would the writer be most likely to say?

 A Famous people should always keep their weddings private.

 B Only photographers should be allowed to attend the ceremony.

 C Getting married in the spotlight ought to be the couple's choice.

 D Being so interested in the lives of people we don't know is wrong.

4 Read the text again and decide if these statements are true (T) or false (F).

1 The writer knows lots of celebrities. ....

2 The writer thinks celebrities' lives are always glamorous. ....

3 What we see of celebrities is not always real. ....

4 Yolanda Burton suggests ways to help couples keep control of their big day. ....

5 The writer feels sorry for celebrities who get married in secret. ....

5 Find words in the article that have these meanings. The first letter of each word is given.

1 attractive, interesting and unusual (para 2): g............................

2 large groups of people (para 3): c............................

3 place (para 3): l............................

4 available only to one person or group of people (para 4): e............................

5 a children's story (para 4): f............................

6 things you remember from the past (para 4): m............................

6 Choose the correct word from Ex 5 to complete the sentences.

1 When buying a house, decide what is most important to you – .... or space.

2 Working on a farm isn't .... but it's rewarding.

3 I like films to have a .... ending.

4 The .... at the new shopping centre were huge.

5 I have the most wonderful .... of my time at summer camp.

6 The .... interview with the pop star was fascinating.

Celebrity weddings

A reader commented on my article from last week. He said it was wrong to be so interested in the weddings of people we don't even know – why do we want to find out all the details of an actor or pop star's big day? I think really it's because we see their faces and read about their lives so often – we feel like we know these people.

At the same time, famous people are like characters in a fairy tale to us. Their lives seem exciting and glamorous. A celebrity wedding is a bit like Cinderella getting married to her prince, and we all want to be there to watch. But we forget that what we see is a public image. They may look perfect but these are actual people, not characters in a story.

Because of all this attention, many celebrities nowadays get married in secret, to keep the crowds of fans and photographers away. But it's not easy to keep the event out of the spotlight. To do this, some celebrities have to hold the ceremony in a faraway location. For instance, actors Michael Fassbender and Alicia Vikander got married on a farm on the island of Ibiza, which was difficult for most photographers to get to.

Yolanda Burton, a celebrity wedding planner I spoke to recently, says she usually advises couples not to 'hide completely'. 'Photos of a secret wedding will be worth thousands of dollars, so photographers will do anything to get them – even use helicopters or drones to take shots from the air!' she said. 'I think the best idea is for the couple to sell exclusive photos to only one magazine. That way, the couple have control over the moments they share. So, the fans get their "fairytale pictures" and the couple also have their own private memories of their wedding day.'

I too love looking at celebrity wedding photos, but I do think it's a shame if you have to hide on your special day. No one should have to worry about that. It's all about respect, really: celebrities or not, the bride and groom should be the ones to decide how to spend the happiest day of their life – and who to share it with.

GRAMMAR

zero, first and second conditionals

1 Complete the zero conditional sentences with the correct form of the verbs in brackets. Then decide which sentences are true for you.

1 When I meet my best friend, she always .... (say), 'What's new?'

2 If I get home too late, my parents .... (be) usually angry.

3 My mum .... (make) me a cake when it's my birthday.

4 It annoys me if anyone .... (go) into my room without asking.

5 If I want to relax, I .... (listen) to music.

6 When my parents .... (have) a busy day, I help make dinner.

2 Complete the first conditional sentences in the conversation. Use the correct form of the verbs in brackets.

Ian

Hi, Dan. I'm on my way, but I'm running a bit late because mum's car broke down. If I ¹............................. (miss) the bus, I ²............................. (let) you know.

Dan

OK. If you ³............................. (not get) here on time, we ⁴............................. (not see) the show because they close the doors. But we can do something different.

Ian

Thanks. If I ⁵............................. (be) too late, ⁶............................. (you / tell) Dylan I'm sorry, please?

Dan

OK. I'm sure he ⁷............................. (understand) the situation if I ⁸............................. (explain) it to him.

3 Choose the correct words to complete the zero and first conditional sentences.

1 If you **want / will want** to take a photo, **you press / you'll press** this button.

2 **I send / I'll send** you an invitation if you **give / will give** me your mobile number.

3 Your mother **is / will be** worried about you if you **don't / won't** call her.

4 If Lily **concentrates / will concentrate**, she always **wins / she'll always win** the game.

5 If you **don't / won't** listen, you **don't / won't** know what to do.

6 You **don't / won't** get to know them if you **don't / won't** talk to them.

4 Read the second conditional sentences from an interview with a child star. Complete them with the correct form of the verbs in brackets.

1 I .... (not be) an actor today if I .... (not enjoy) it.

2 They .... (tell) me if I .... (need) to take a break.

3 If I .... (have) children, I .... (not push) them to be actors.

4 If I .... (not be) an actor, I .... (miss) the excitement a lot.

5 If I .... (can) work with any actor, it .... (be) Eddie Redmayne.

6 I .... (not want) to be in a musical if I .... (have to) dance.

7 My brother says he .... (be) in films if he .... (not be) a musician.

5 🔊 5.1 Listen to the interview and check your answers.

6 Complete the interview with the correct form of the verbs in brackets.

What would you do IF...?

Every week at Pop News we invite our readers to ask their favourite celebrity the question 'What would you do if ... ?' This week we say hi to Billy from the band IDX.

Hi, Billy! What would you do if you ¹............................. (not be) in a pop group?

Ah, a difficult question! If I ²............................. (not sing), I'd be really bored. Singing is my passion.

If you won the lottery, what ³............................. (you / buy)?

Great question! If I ⁴............................. (have) lots of money, I'd buy a big house for my family.

Billy, if you had another pet, what ⁵............................. (it / be)?

Well, I've already got two dogs, but if I ⁶............................. (get) another pet, it'd be a snake.

We know you hate flying, Billy. So what would you do if the band ⁷............................. (want) to do a concert in another country?

Well, if it wasn't too far, I ⁸............................. (travel) by train. I love trains.

VOCABULARY

entertainment

1 Which of these verbs comes before all the words in each group?

book   clap   entertain   film   interview   perform   review

1	loudly	your hands	for a long time
2	a scene	a TV programme	a documentary
3	on stage	in a play	on TV
4	people	the crowd	the audience
5	a film star	a director	a politician
6	a ticket	a seat	a holiday
7	a concert	a book	a TV programme

2 🔊 5.2 What is each person going to do? Listen and match the activities (A–F) with the conversations (1–6).

A perform in a ballet ....

B record a song ....

C interview a pop star ....

D film a news report ....

E review a film ....

F book a practice room ....

3 Look at the pictures and complete the crossword.

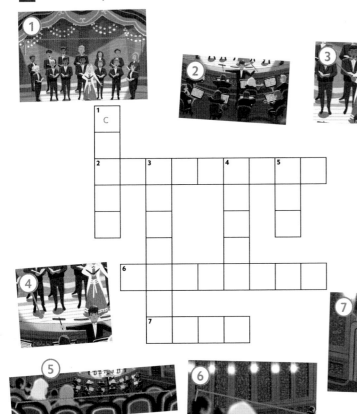

4 Complete the blog post with words from Activity 3 in the correct form. Use one word in each gap.

goodtheatreblog.com

My local theatre is only small, but it's got
¹ .... of big, comfortable seats
that are great for relaxing and enjoying
shows. Tonight the ² .... was full
of students who came to watch a
musical by the Creative Teens Theatre
Company. A live ³ ....
played music during the show and a
⁴ .... sang a mixture of classical
and pop music. When the show
finished, the performers came back on
⁵ .... and continued for another
half hour. Everything was great about the
show except for the ⁶ ....
The actors looked hot and very
uncomfortable all night.

Extend

5 Match the jobs (1–7) with the actions (A–G) to make sentences.

1 A poet

2 A film-maker

3 A disc jockey

4 A musician

5 A journalist

6 An author

7 A performer

A writes books.

B plays songs on the radio or at a disco.

C writes poems.

D entertains people.

E writes articles or reports.

F plays an instrument or sings.

G makes movies.

6 Complete the questions with these words.

animation   clip   exhibition   fiction   poem

When was the last time you:

1 read or wrote a .... ?

2 watched a video .... ?

3 read some .... ?

4 went to an .... ?

5 watched an .... ?

7 Answer the questions in Ex 6.

LISTENING

1 🔊 **5.3 You will hear six conversations about music. Listen and match the conversations (1–6) to the topics (A–F).**

Which conversation is about:

A listening to live music? ....

B a band's new album? ....

C listening to music while travelling? ....

D practising for a music performance? ....

E listening to music with headphones? ....

F classical music? ....

2 e 🔊 **5.4 Listen again. For each question, choose the correct answer.**

1 You will hear a girl talking about listening to music in her car. Why does she do it?

    A to help her concentrate

    B to stop her from feeling ill

    C to make a journey go more quickly

2 You will hear two friends talking about a concert. They agree that

    A the band didn't play very well.

    B one of the performances was longer than they expected.

    C they were standing too far from the stage.

3 You will hear two friends talking about listening to music on a smartphone. What do they agree about it?

    A The sound quality isn't good with headphones.

    B Listening to music uses up a lot of battery.

    C Using headphones is polite.

4 You will hear two friends talking about an album they listened to. The girl thinks that the second song

    A is very original.

    B has good words.

    C sounds like one by another artist.

5 You will hear two friends talking about listening to music while studying. What does the boy say about it?

    A He only does it with certain subjects.

    B It helps his memory.

    C He is careful not to disturb other people.

6 You will hear a girl talking about a music competition she has entered. How does she feel?

    A nervous about performing in public

    B unsure she can win

    C worried because she hasn't practised enough

unless, in case, if I were you

3 Rewrite the sentences using *unless*.

1 We won't wait for them if they don't call to say they're coming.

    ....

2 I won't go to the cinema if you don't come too.

    ....

3 We'll stop and have lunch if you aren't too busy.

    ....

4 If Jo doesn't have to look after her sister, she'll join us.

    ....

5 We'll eat later if you aren't hungry.

    ....

4 Choose the correct words to complete the review.

SPACE RAT III

Reader rating ★ ☆ ☆ ☆ ☆

The latest in the Space Rat series has nothing new to say. **¹Unless / If** you haven't seen it yet, all I can say is, 'Don't bother!'

The film starts with a scene on Matt's spaceship, which you won't understand **²unless / if** you've seen Space Rat II. At least the special effects are exciting. The problem is that the film gets worse from then on. If I **³am / were** you, I **⁴will / would** stay at home and watch the first two films on DVD. At least they have a storyline and are entertaining. I wouldn't waste money on a ticket for this film, **⁵unless / if** I needed some help falling asleep!

⁶If / Unless you are planning on seeing the film at the cinema, take a large coffee **⁷in case / unless** you feel your eyes closing, as mine did. Give it a miss.

5 🔊 **5.5 Complete the conversation with these words and phrases. Listen and check your answers.**

if   if I were   in case   unless   you are   you aren't

A: Have you signed up for guitar lessons?

B: Yes, I have. Have you?

A: Yeah. Are you going to buy a guitar or rent one?

B: I've rented one already. Then **¹**.......................... I don't like the classes, I can just return it.

A: That's a good idea. I'll rent one too, **²**.......................... I give up after a while. Where did you get yours from?

B: The music shop in town. I'd go there and try some different sizes **³**.......................... you. Then you'll get the best one for you.

A: Oh! I'll enjoy that. I always thought that you can't go in unless **⁴**.......................... a real musician. Are all the guitars the same price?

B: Yes, they are, **⁵**.......................... you choose a very fancy one.

A: Will you come with me tomorrow and help me choose, if **⁶**.......................... busy?

B: OK. It'll be fun!

SPEAKING

1 Put these words for describing things in the correct group.

black   brown   leather   metal   orange   plastic
round   small   thin   wood

size and shape	colour	material

2 Look at the photos and put the letters in the correct order to complete the descriptions. The words are from Ex 1.

① ② ③

1 It looks like two spoons. It's made of .... (odow) and it's .... (mlsal). You use it for playing music.

2 It's a thing you use for cleaning flutes. It's long and .... (ntih). It's made of .... (amtel) and .... (lpsiact).

3 It's a thing which you use to carry a musical instrument. It's made of .... (elaehrt) and it's .... (lbcka).

3 🔊 5.6 Listen to the questions and answer them using the pictures and information in Ex 2. Record yourself.

4 🔊 5.7 Listen to your recording from Ex 3. Then listen to track 5.7. Compare. How are they similar or different?

5 Look at the photo and complete the description with these words. There are three words you do not need.

for   kind   looks   made
make   small   thing   to

It's ¹............................ and cute. It's ²............................ of porcelain and I think someone has painted it by hand. It ³............................ like a bird, but actually it's a ⁴............................ of toy that makes a sound. You can't use it ⁵............................ play music, though, because it has only one hole at the top so it doesn't make different sounds. I think it's beautiful.

6 🔊 5.8 Complete the conversation with one word in each gap. Listen and check your answers.

A: What ¹............................ happening in this photo? Is one of those boys your brother?

B: No, that's Aidan, my cousin. He lives in Ireland. He's the one with long hair. I think he's playing in some ²............................ of street music festival in this picture.

A: What's he playing? It looks ³............................ a drum, but he's holding it differently.

B: Yes, it is a type of drum. I can't ⁴............................ what it's called, but it's an Irish instrument.

A: What's it ⁵............................ of?

B: Wood and animal skin, I think. You use that little stick ⁶............................ hit it, but you can use your fingers, too. Aidan can play it really quickly.

A: It looks like fun.

B: Yeah. I need to ask him to let me try next time I visit.

45

WRITING

an article

1 Read the comments from some students' film and TV programme reviews. Are they positive (P) or negative (N)?

1 I was really disappointed with the film. ....

2 The story was fascinating. ....

3 It was a really exciting show. ....

4 I was bored by the end of the film. ....

5 It was a very interesting series. ....

6 The special effects were disappointing. ....

2 Rewrite these negative comments. Use these adjectives and *a bit*.

boring   cold   expensive   old   sad

1 The concert wasn't very interesting.

....

2 The ending of the film wasn't very happy.

....

3 It wasn't very warm in the theatre.

....

4 The tickets weren't very cheap.

....

5 The songs don't sound very new.

....

3 Read the advert. What two things can you write about?

.... or ....

Music to our ears

As part of our music project, we want to know what everyone is listening to now! Tell us about your favourite new playlist or a live music performance you watched recently.

- How did you hear about it?
- What is / was the best thing about it?
- Is / Was there anything that isn't / wasn't so good?

4 Look at your answers to Ex 3. Do you need to write about both of these things?

....

5 Complete a student's article with these words and phrases.

best thing   hear it   only bad thing
on the whole   perfect for   recommend

Cool it!
by Emma Bower

My favourite new playlist is called 'Cool it!' and it's got a great mix of relaxing songs on it. I downloaded it because my best friend told me about it. I'm glad she did!

The ¹......................... about the playlist is the third song, 'After the storm'. It's amazing! It's by a new artist called Rachel Roberts. Rachel's got a great a voice and her music is ²......................... playing when you're studying. When you ³........................., I'm sure you'll become a Rachel Roberts fan.

The ⁴......................... about the playlist is some of the songs at the end aren't very relaxing! But ⁵........................., I would ⁶......................... this playlist because the first 20 songs are fantastic.

6 Read the article again and choose the things the student does.

1 use a title ☐

2 cover all three questions in the advert ☐

3 make positive comments ☐

4 describe problems ☐

5 make a recommendation ☐

6 describe other people's opinions ☐

7 Read the advert in Ex 3 again. Decide what you are going to write about and make notes to plan your answer. Try to do the things you ticked in Ex 6.

8 🄴 Write your article in about 100 words. Use your notes from Ex 7 to help you.

UNIT CHECK

1 Choose the correct verb forms to complete the sentences.

1 If I win the tickets to the festival, **I take / I'll take** you with me.

2 If you practise a lot, you **will / would** learn the dance routine.

3 The theatre will lose money if they **don't / won't** sell all the tickets.

4 Piano players only get better if they **play / will play** every day.

5 You'll learn faster if **you practise / you'll practise** more.

6 If you need help with the scenery, **ask / you'll ask** me.

7 You won't hear their most famous songs if **you leave / you'll leave** early.

2 Complete the second conditional sentences with the correct form of the verbs in brackets.

1 If we .... (ask) them, ... (they / sing) for us?

2 I .... (not play) the drums in here if I .... (be) you.

3 Jake and Skye .... (go) to the concert if they .... (have) tickets.

4 If you .... (like) the music, ... (you / dance) with me?

5 You .... (love) this festival if you .... (be) here.

6 What .... (you / do) if you .... (lose) your phone?

7 I .... (not go) on a talent show even if someone .... (ask) me.

8 How .... (you / feel) if you .... (meet) your favourite pop star?

3 Complete the advice with *in case, if I were you* or *unless*.

1 Take a bottle of water .... there aren't any drinks.

2 Don't leave your seat .... you want to lose it.

3 I wouldn't sit in the first row .... because the view isn't very good.

4 ...., I would ask for my money back.

5 Can I have your mobile number .... I need to call you?

6 You should wear a jacket .... it gets colder in the evening.

7 I'd study music .... You could be a professional musician.

8 .... you say something, she'll never know you like her.

4 Complete the blog post with these words. There are three words you do not need.

---

audience   choir   costumes   musicians   orchestra
performers   rows   seats   stage

The last day of our holiday – **it was the best!**

On Sunday we were very lucky because there was a circus event in the city. We saw some fantastic street [1]........................... doing acrobatics and mime! There were also [2]........................... in every square, playing folk songs.

After lunch it started to rain, so we went to an exhibition of traditional local [3]........................... . They looked amazing – but very uncomfortable!

And in the evening we went to a rather unusual concert, where the [4]........................... played using instruments made of recycled plastic! Unbelievable! We had good [5]..........................., near the [6]..........................., so I took some great photos – I'll post them tomorrow.

5 e Read the review. Choose the correct answers to complete the review.

Stars of the **future**

This week, *Entertainment News* is .... The Voice, Saturday night's favourite talent show.

It's a simple idea. The contestant comes onto the [1]........ and gives a short introduction. Then the studio [2]........ watches as he or she sings in front of four judges. The judges can't see who is [3]........ because they have their backs to the singer. If they like the singer, they press a red button and their chair turns around. When this happens, everybody starts [4]........ because it means the singer is good. The winner of the competition has the chance to [5]........ an album. The show works well because the singers are good and also because the judges and other guest stars know how to [6]........ the audience with stories of how they became famous.

	A	B	C
	A interviewing	B performing	C reviewing
1	A row	B stage	C exit
2	A audience	B choir	C orchestra
3	A performing	B filming	C acting
4	A recording	B clapping	C entertaining
5	A act	B perform	C record
6	A interview	B review	C entertain

READING

1 Read the clues and complete the crossword.

Across

2 something you can see

5 continue to live after serious problems or a dangerous situation

6 Earth, Mercury, Mars, etc.

Down

1 travel around an area to find out about it

3 great; so good that you can't believe it

4 very small

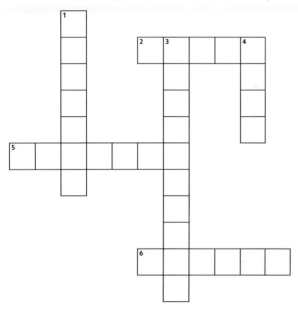

2 Read the advertisement. What do the pronouns in bold (1–6) refer to? Circle the right part of the text.

Scuba diving lessons

Are you interested in discovering life underwater? Would you like to explore the ocean and see **¹its** magic for yourself? Take a scuba diving lesson with us and do just **²that**.

Our expert instructors will take you to a fantastic spot in the ocean. First, **³they'll** teach you about safety as **⁴this** is extremely important to us. Then **⁵they'll** show you some amazing sea life. You'll even be able to photograph **⁶it** with one of our underwater cameras.

Click here to book a lesson. **⁷It's** the experience of a lifetime!

3 Read the blog post on page 49 quickly. Was the writer's experience positive or negative?

....

4 Find the pronouns in these sentences (A–H). Sometimes there is more than one.

A It was calm and warm.

B They were a real surprise.

C I didn't want to return to land, though.

D I didn't think it would be possible.

E Then we went down further.

F There were four other beginners with me.

G I wasn't quite sure if it was right.

H They were really painful.

5 **e** Read the blog post again. For each gap, choose the correct sentence from Ex 4. There are three extra sentences which you do not need to use. Use the pronouns you identified in Ex 4 to help you find which sentence fits each gap.

6 Find words in the article that have these meanings.

1 very surprised (para 2) ....

2 immediately, without delay (para 3) ....

3 moving in a regular rhythm (para 3) ....

4 feel so frightened you can't think clearly (para 3) ....

5 relax (para 3) ....

6 the top part of an area of water or land (para 5) ....

7 Choose the right word from Ex 6 to complete the sentences from reviews of a scuba diving trip.

1 You can hear your heart .... because it's so quiet down there.

2 It's easy to .... at first, but once you .... you'll love it.

3 You have to remember not to swim .... up to the ....

4 I was .... at everything we saw – incredible!

My first scuba diving experience

I've wanted to scuba dive since I was little. I saw a documentary about the ocean and I wanted to go underwater and see all those amazing sea creatures myself. **1**............................ . However, last week my dream came true and I went scuba diving for the first time.

I was on holiday with my parents on my birthday. My gift was a scuba diving lesson. I was amazed! It wasn't a solo lesson. **2**............................ . They were all as excited as me. Thomas, the instructor, started by teaching us how to breathe with the equipment. He taught us what to do and also what not to do. At that point, I started to get nervous. I realised scuba diving could be dangerous.

A lot of beginners start in the swimming pool but we went straight into the sea. The boat took us to a place about fifteen minutes from the coast. There, we got into the water. **3**............................ . My body wasn't. My heart was beating fast and I suddenly felt cold. I was starting to panic. I took some deep breaths and tried to calm down.

We were shown some breathing exercises to start, then we went down into the water. We got down to about ten metres. I could only pay attention to my ears at first. **4**............................ . I tried to get the water out of them and after a minute or two, they stopped hurting. I looked around. The sea was a beautiful colour – not the same as it looked from the boat at all. There were fish all around me. They were all different colours. I started to relax.

We spent around forty-five minutes in the sea before the instructor told us to swim slowly up to the surface so we could head back to the coast. **5**............................ . I wanted to stay there longer to enjoy the fascinating sea life but sadly the day had come to an end. If you ever get the chance to dive, you should take it. I loved it and I'm definitely planning on going again next year. I just have to save some money now!

GRAMMAR

the passive

1 Choose the correct verb forms to complete the passive sentences.

1 The sand on the beach **is / are** cleaned every morning.
2 All of the children in this class were **including / included** in the documentary.
3 This fruit **isn't / aren't** used for cooking because it tastes disgusting.
4 The waterfall is often **photographed / photograph** at night.
5 The tickets for the trip **weren't / didn't** included in the price of the holiday.
6 The soil **hasn't / wasn't** prepared for the new plants, so nothing grew well.
7 Your help **isn't needed / doesn't need** at the moment, but thank you for offering.
8 The forest plants are **using / used** to make medicine.

2 🔊 6.1 Complete the news report with these passive verbs. Listen and check your answers.

is often hit   is still covered   was hit   was moved   were asked
were given   were provided   were reported

Resort hit by avalanche

The Mountain View Resort **¹**........................... by a small avalanche yesterday. Guests **²**........................... to stay in their rooms for several hours while the emergency services tried to reach them. They **³**........................... food and drinks by hotel staff, and children **⁴**........................... with games. As this is an area which **⁵**........................... by avalanches, locals were able to keep guests calm. Everyone in the area **⁶**........................... out of the resort during the evening and no missing people or serious injuries **⁷**........................... . The area **⁸**........................... in large amounts of snow, and hotels will remain closed for at least a week.

3 Complete the sentences with the correct passive form of the verbs in brackets.

1 All tourists .... (warn) to leave the beach when there's a red flag.
2 The children .... (not teach) in the villages where they live.
3 This photo .... (take) when we were in India.
4 More help .... (need) if we are going to change this situation.
5 The rubbish bags .... (collect) earlier this morning.
6 Dangerous animals .... (not use) in the documentary we saw.
7 The river .... (clean) by volunteers every year.
8 Those small houses .... (build) by our grandparents many years ago.

4 Read the email and complete the sentences (1–5) using the present simple or past simple passive. Look at the verbs in bold to help you.

Hi Charlotte,

I'm staying in an amazing village in Tenerife. Because it's hidden behind some huge mountains, people didn't know about it for years. When tourists finally **¹discovered** it in the 1960s, locals **²built** new houses and cafés there. Unfortunately, young people **³don't need** the new houses because they are leaving the village to work in the city. But lots of tourists **⁴visit** the village all the time. A good new road **⁵links** the village to the airport, so it's easy for them to come and go.

See you soon.

Aiden

1 It .... by tourists in the 1960s.
2 New houses and cafés .... there.
3 The new houses .... by young people because they're leaving the village.
4 The village .... by lots of tourists every year.
5 The village .... to the airport by a good new road.

5 Write a short paragraph about a place you know well. If you don't know all of the information, make it up. Make sure you include:

• what it is called.
• where it is located.
• when it was built or discovered and who by.
• who it is visited by.
• what people think of it.

VOCABULARY

the natural world

1 Match the word halves (1–8) with (A–H) to form words about the natural world.

1 pa........
2 fo........
3 wa........
4 st........
5 fi........
6 sa........
7 cl........
8 ro........

A nd
B ar
C ve
D ck
E eld
F th
G g
H oud

2 Complete the sentences with the correct form of the words from Ex 1. Use a plural form where necessary.

1 Max and his friends couldn't go surfing because the .... weren't big enough.
2 We couldn't see very far in front of us because of the ....
3 I didn't want to cycle on the road, so I took the .... along the river instead.
4 Grace and her friend were relaxing in the sun when they saw the dark .... in the distance.
5 There's only one .... in the sky tonight!
6 It's so hot at the beach today, it's impossible to walk on the ....

3 Complete the advert with these words.

cliff   paths   sand   stars   sunshine   waterfall   waves

Island Adventure Centre

Come on your own or come with friends. With around 325 days of ¹............................ every year, you won't be bored at Island Adventure Centre! You can surf the ²............................ , play beach volleyball on the soft white ³............................ or join us on an exciting midnight walk along one of the beautiful mountain ⁴............................ that lead to the highest ⁵............................ in Turkey. Our adventure centre is located on the top of a ⁶............................ , with amazing views of the mountains behind and the sea in front. In the evenings we also offer boat trips with music, so you can dance all night and watch the ⁷............................ in the sky at the same time!

For more information, visit our website.

4 Match the first part of the sentences (1–7) with the correct ending (A–G).

1 They live in a beautiful,
2 Marie's making a wonderful
3 She's wearing a strange
4 They're swimming in a dangerous,
5 We're looking up at the incredible,
6 I took a walk on the unusual,
7 Harry followed the scary,

A blue coat.
B white stars.
C old house.
D black sand.
E deep lake.
F long path.
G chocolate cake.

5 Choose the correct answers to complete the blog post.

The power of the sea

We all love watching the ¹........ waves at the beach and some of us can even surf in them, but on a recent geography trip I discovered just how powerful the sea really is. When it's very windy, strong waves hit the ²........ , and the power of the water breaks up the ³........ , which falls and creates the beach below. Sometimes you get a ⁴........ beach, but in some areas the ⁵........ is black because the beach is near a volcano. Strong ⁶........ can then pull what's on the beach back into the sea. In some areas, this is causing a problem because plants are dying because the ⁷........ that they live in is being carried away by the wind and waves.

1 A big, amazing   B big and amazing   C amazing, big
2 A paths   B cliffs   C clouds
3 A rock   B earth   C sand
4 A beautiful, white B white, beautiful C white and beautiful
5 A field   B sand   C fog
6 A snowfall   B sunshine   C waves
7 A fog   B earth   C storm

Extend

6 🔊 6.2 Match the adjectives in A with the nouns in B. Listen and check your answers. Listen again and repeat.

A   clear   green   heavy   humid   narrow   sandy   strong   thick

B   beach   fog   grass   path   sky   snowfall   waves   weather

7 Write a paragraph describing an area of natural beauty you know. Try to use words from this page.

LISTENING

1 🔊 6.3 Listen to a radio interview with a boy who organised an event. Choose the correct words to complete the sentences.

1 Lucas organised a **marathon** / **rubbish** run.

2 There were **200** / **300** runners in the race.

3 The event **was** / **wasn't** successful.

4 Lucas **wants** / **doesn't want** to organise the event again.

2 Read the questions (1–6) and find the key words.

1 Why did Lucas decide to organise the event?
  A to make his parents proud of him
  B to improve the appearance of his local area
  C to try to win a prize

2 On the day of the event, Lucas was
  A concerned about tiny details.
  B confident that it would go well.
  C excited to take part in it.

3 What did people love most about the event?
  A that they had a fun time
  B that the whole family could attend
  C how it was organised

4 For next year's event, Lucas will
  A ask people to provide their own equipment.
  B allow people to run the race in teams.
  C choose a different day.

5 What does Lucas want to do in the future?
  A help other teenagers organise events
  B create similar events across the country
  C learn to use social media to advertise the event

6 What advice does Lucas give to other young people?
  A Try to make a small difference to your area.
  B Pick up your rubbish and put it in a bin.
  C Be creative with your ideas.

3 🔊 6.4 Listen again. For each question in Ex 2, choose the correct answer.

have / get something done

4 Put the words in the correct order to make sentences.

1 had / her / she / hair / cut / Paul / by

....

2 this afternoon / I / to / my / get / bike / want / repaired

....

3 do / eyes / you / your / where / tested / have?

....

4 my / I'm / invitations / printed / having

....

5 not / I'm / getting / coloured / my / hair

....

6 checked / we / the / last week / got / computer

....

7 we / our nails / at the salon / done / had

....

8 a dress / Becky's / for her sister's wedding / made / getting

....

5 Complete the sentences with the correct form of the verbs in brackets. Use the present simple, present continuous or past simple of *have something done*.

1 I .... my eyes .... every year. (check)

2 They .... their skateboards .... in the shop yesterday. (repair)

3 Emma .... her photo .... at the moment. (take)

4 Daniel always .... his hair .... by his dad. (cut)

5 They .... pizza .... last night. (deliver)

6 We .... the classrooms .... last year. (not paint)

7 My neighbours .... their house .... twice a week. (clean)

8 My grandma .... her hearing .... last week and it was fine. (test)

SPEAKING

1 🔊 6.5 Listen to the instructions. Match the options (1–5) with the pictures (A–E).

1 charge for plastic bags at the cafeteria ....

2 students bring their own reusable water bottles for drinking ....

3 the school provides more recycling bins ....

4 coffee is served in mugs, not plastic cups ....

5 the school provides free drinking water ....

Reducing plastic waste

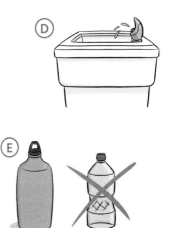

2 🔊 6.6 Listen to two students doing the task in Ex 1 and answer the questions.

1 Which options do they discuss? ....

2 Which student tries to help the other say more? ....

3 Complete the gaps in the conversation (1–5) with sentences A–F. There is one extra sentence you do not need.

A Go on.

B Why do you think that?

C Do you agree?

D How would that help?

E What do you think about the mugs?

F What do you like?

A: I think the school should provide recycling bins. **¹**........

B: Yes, I do. Um … er …

A: **²**........

B: Yes, well, we definitely need to recycle more, and having more recycling bins will help.

A: Exactly. **³**........

B: They're better than throw away cups with plastic lids. The cafeteria should use those, really. Plastic lids are a waste and can't be recycled easily.

A: I agree, and we use so many of them. I also think the school needs to provide more water fountains, too. Then people won't need to buy bottles of water.

B: Yes, that's a good idea. And so is charging for plastic bags in the cafeteria, in my opinion.

A: Hmm … **⁴**........

B: Well, if people had to pay, they'd stop using them.

A: **⁵**........

B: Because we only use them when they're free!

A: Hmm, good point!

4 🔊 6.7 Listen again and check your answers.

5 Read the questions. Choose the best phrase to answer each one.

Because they …   For me, … is better because …
Well, firstly, we …   Yes, I would because …
Yes, they ought to …

---

1 When you buy a drink, do you prefer a glass bottle or a plastic one?

....

2 Would you like to use less plastic?

....

3 In what ways do we use a lot of plastic?

....

4 Why do you think people use so many plastic bags?

....

5 Do you think schools should recycle more?

....

6 🔊 6.8 Listen to the questions from Ex 5 and record your answers. Listen to your answers. Did you give enough details?

6 Down to earth

WRITING

an email

1 Read the writing task. Why is Elspeth writing?

A to thank you for something   **C** to accept an invitation

B to invite you to do something

> Read this email from your English-speaking friend Elspeth and the notes you have made. Write your email using all the notes. Write your answer in about 100 words.

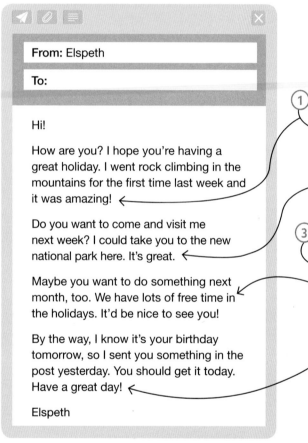

From: Elspeth

To:

Hi!

How are you? I hope you're having a great holiday. I went rock climbing in the mountains for the first time last week and it was amazing! ←

Do you want to come and visit me next week? I could take you to the new national park here. It's great. ←

Maybe you want to do something next month, too. We have lots of free time in the holidays. It'd be nice to see you!

By the way, I know it's your birthday tomorrow, so I sent you something in the post yesterday. You should get it today. Have a great day! ←

Elspeth

1 Respond to this news.

2 Refuse and say why.

3 Yes! Invite Elspeth to my home.

4 Thank her.

2 Put the words in the correct order to make useful phrases for your email.

1 visiting / about / me / in August / how?

....

2 for / me / sending / thank / a birthday / you / gift

....

3 visit / I / can't / I'm / next week / you / afraid

....

4 would you / come and stay /next month / with me / like to?

....

5 sounds / idea / like / a great / that

....

6 come / I'd / and see / next week / love to / you

....

3 Decide if the phrases in Ex 2 give thanks (T), make an invitation (M), accept an invitation (A) or refuse an invitation (R).

1 ....   **3** ....   **5** ....

2 ....   **4** ....   **6** ....

4 Plan your answer to the writing task in Ex 1. Follow these steps.

1 Find the four main points you need to include.

2 Think about what you can write for each point. Make notes.

3 Think about useful phrases you can use to thank, invite, etc. Add them to your notes.

4 Think about how you will start and end your email.

....
....
....
....
....
....
....
....
....
....

5 **e** Write your email in about 100 words. Use your notes from Ex 4.

UNIT CHECK

1 Complete the puzzle with the past participles of the verbs. What is the infinitive of the past participle in red?

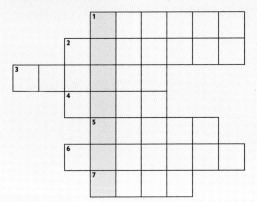

Across

1 break   5 give

2 write   6 think

3 throw   7 tear

4 sing   infinitive: ....

2 Use some of the past participles from Ex 1 to complete the sentences in the passive.

1 The girl .... lots of new toys for her birthday.

2 She returned the item to the shop and told them it .... when she opened it.

3 His speech .... on his tablet – but his tablet is in that taxi!

4 None of the students knew how the book .... but the teacher was furious.

5 Every year the plants .... inside when it gets cold, but they still don't always survive the winter.

3 Choose the correct verb forms to complete the sentences.

1 Experts believe that the avalanche was **cause / caused** by the change in temperature.

2 The bags at our local supermarket **isn't make / aren't made** of plastic. They're paper bags.

3 The rocks over there were **forming / formed** over millions of years.

4 A lot of rubbish **was found / were founded** on the beach this morning.

5 That photo **didn't take / wasn't taken** in Paris! That's a street in Rome.

6 Ben and Hannah **were / have** warned about the river, but still went swimming.

7 The animals at the zoo **are given / were gave** food several times each day.

8 The moon **has covers / is covered** by the clouds, so we can't see it.

4 Complete the words in the messages. The first and last letter of each word is given.

> Hi! Got here late last night but luckily there was a full **¹**m...........................n, so we could see to put the tent up.

> Great!

> We could see hundreds of **²**s...........................s in the sky. It was amazing!

> How's the weather?

> Warm and not a **³**c...........................d in the sky this morning. Hope this **⁴**s...........................e lasts, but the campsite owner says it'll be windy tomorrow. We might even get a **⁵**s...........................m by the end of the week!

> Hope not! What are you doing today?

> We're going for a walk. There's a **⁶**p...........................h that goes along the mountain. It'll take us to a **⁷**w...........................l about five kilometres away, where we hope to swim.

> Sounds amazing!

> Yeah, it does. I think the water will be pretty cold, though.

5 Write these adjectives in the correct group in the table.

amazing ancient dangerous flat high horrible huge
incredible narrow pretty scary tiny

opinion	fact

6 Find and correct mistakes with the order of adjectives in four of the sentences.

1 Rob found a smooth, comfortable rock and sat on it.

....

2 They had their picnic on the lovely, green grass in the park.

....

3 We spent the day at the sandy, pretty beach.

....

4 We sat and looked at the beautiful, calm sea.

....

5 We watched the pink, amazing sunrise.

....

6 No one went into the icy, scary river.

....

REVIEW: UNITS 1–6

1 Choose the correct verb forms to complete the text.

George and I ¹**are / has been / have been** friends for a long time. We ²**met / were meeting / have met** at summer camp five years ago and we still ³**got on / get on / are getting on** well today. We ⁴**spent / have spent / are spending** a lot of time together since we ⁵**met / have met / were meeting**, but last year we ⁶**didn't see / haven't seen / weren't seeing** each other at all because George moved to a different area with his family. We ⁷**meet up / 're meeting up / 've met up** with each other next month. We ⁸**'ll probably see / 'll see probably / 're probably seeing** a football match. We ⁹**already planned / 've already planned / 've already planning** to go to a summer camp next year, but we ¹⁰**didn't decide / weren't deciding / haven't decided** where we'll go yet.

2 Complete the texts with these words.

calm   captain   competes   confident   hits   kick   lose
score   scores   serious   trains   wins

Roger is a great tennis player. He's fast, athletic and he ¹........................... the ball hard. He's ²........................... in his abilities because he knows he's one of the best players in our school. He doesn't ³........................... a lot of matches. What's funny, though, is that he's terrible at football – he can't ⁴........................... a ball!

Gareth is a brilliant footballer. He ⁵........................... a lot of goals. He's always ⁶........................... when he plays and not at all stressed. His team usually ⁷........................... their matches because he's a good ⁸........................... .

Simone is a fantastic gymnast. She ⁹........................... very hard in the gym every day and is ¹⁰........................... about her work. When she ¹¹........................... in tournaments, she often gets the highest ¹²........................... .

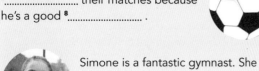

3 Complete the conversations with the correct form of the verbs in brackets.

Conversation 1

If somebody ¹........................... (buy) you a ticket to anywhere in the world, where would you want to go?

I'd go to New York. I ²........................... (dream) about it now and then.

If you ³........................... (can) take a friend, who ⁴........................... (it / be)?

Definitely Phoebe. She ⁵........................... (come) with me and my family to Spain last year and we ⁶........................... (have) lots of fun.

Conversation 2

If the weather ⁷........................... (be) nice tomorrow, what will you do?

I ⁸........................... (take) my dog to the beach. What about you?

I ⁹........................... (go) to my grandparent's house unless they ¹⁰........................... (have) other plans. Last month I went round to see them but they ¹¹........................... (hike) in the hills!

Conversation 3

What happens if someone ¹²........................... (press) that button there?

I've got no idea. No one ever does it. Try it and see!

Um, no! I ¹³........................... (not do) it just in case something bad ¹⁴........................... (happen)!

4 Choose the correct word to complete the sentences.

1 We tried to **book / perform / review** some seats for the theatre, but there weren't any left.

2 Emma's rock band is going to **entertain / film / record** an album this summer.

3 I don't understand this word. Can you explain what it **repeats / means / translates**?

4 I always sit near the front **exit / row / stage** at the theatre so that I can see everything.

5 I need to **plug in / turn on / set up** my phone. The battery's nearly gone.

6 I've got to **interview / perform / review** this book for my English class, but I haven't read it yet.

7 Jake put his clothes in the **court / locker / track** and went into the pool.

8 Sorry, can you **pronounce / repeat / say** that again?

5 Complete the sentences with the correct active or passive form of the verbs in brackets. Use the present simple or past simple.

1 Photos of the students .... (always / take) on the last day of school.
2 The students .... (spend) yesterday making plans for the summer.
3 A prize .... (give) to the best student yesterday.
4 One of the students .... (film) last night's concert.
5 The science students .... (take) to the science museum last week.
6 Uniforms .... (not wear) by students on the last day.
7 A party for students .... (organise) by the teachers every year.
8 The students .... (perform) a play each December.

6 Complete the email with these words.

audience	cliff	cloud	entertainment	path
sand	storm	sunshine	waves	wetsuit

Hi Anna,

I'm having a brilliant time in Cuba. After the bad ¹............................ last night with rain and wind, today the weather is great with lots of ²............................ – there isn't a ³............................ in the sky.

The hotel is great. It's on the top of a ⁴............................ and the view is amazing. The staff are lovely. There's ⁵............................ every evening, which is fun. Last night there was an amazing singer with his guitar. The night before we watched some dancers. Some of the ⁶............................ joined in but we didn't. We just watched.

Behind the hotel there's a ⁷............................ that you can take to walk down to the beach. The sea is an incredible colour and the ⁸............................ is soft and white. This afternoon we're hoping to go surfing because there are some great ⁹............................ . I won't need to wear a ¹⁰............................ because the water's so warm. It's not like home at all!

See you soon,

Max

7 Put the words in the correct order to make sentences and questions.

1 up / black / they / and saw / clouds / big, / looked / some
2 on / can / the lights / turn / you?
3 a goal / the match / but lost / the team / scored
4 word / how / pronounce / you / do / this?
5 strawberry / all of / cake / they / lovely / ate / that
6 the children / on stage / perform / we / the play / watched
7 a dress / for the party / having / Jessica / made / is
8 clapped / the orchestra / when / we / finished / loudly

8 **e** For each question, choose the correct answer.

Nature and sports technology

Researchers are using nature to help them create better sports technology. This is because animals and plants are ¹........ at adapting to the world around them. When there's a problem, they find a solution. Studying these living things can ²........ us about how they move, which can help sportspeople to ³........ better.

One example is listening to the heartbeat of animals to find out when they speed up and when they slow down. If athletes ⁴........ up an app to measure their heartbeats, they can learn when to go fast and when to go slow when they ⁵........ against others. This will help them to ⁶........ more events.

One animal has already helped to make skis safer. The gecko lizard can stick to trees. Scientists have examined how it does this and used this knowledge to make skis safer in icy conditions.

	A	**B**	**C**	**D**
1	keen	brilliant	interested	intelligent
2	talk	say	tell	understand
3	train	coach	know	teach
4	turn	set	give	keep
5	race	join	meet	enter
6	beat	win	lose	compete

7 Travellers' tales

READING

1 Complete the blog post with the correct form of these verbs.

get about   jumped off   jumped on   signed up   stop off

My classmates and I have just had a fun day in London. We went on a 'duck tour' of the city in a vehicle that's half-boat, half-truck. It's a great way to ¹............................ and see the city from both road and river. We ²............................ the truck near the London Eye and travelled past all the main sights like Big Ben. After a while, the vehicle went straight from the road down into the Thames, where we travelled up the river to see where James Bond and other spies live! We ³............................ the boat at the London Eye and walked back to our hotel. Some of us ⁴............................ for an ice cream on the way. And for tomorrow, we've all ⁵............................ for a trip to Madame Tussauds to see the wax models of famous people. I can't wait!

2 These young people (1–5) are going to take a course at a language school in the UK. They all want to stay with a host family during their visit. Read text 1 about Sofia quickly. What information is given about her?

family life ☐   interests ☐
food preferences ☐   room preferences ☐
friends ☐

Sofia loves watching sports. She enjoys cooking and wants to try local dishes but she doesn't usually eat sweet things. She's happy to share a room with another language school student.

Luca is really active. He loves all sports and wants to ride a bike to school. He'd like to share a room with another language school student. He dislikes spicy food.

3 On page 59 there are descriptions of eight host families. Read description A. Which of these things are mentioned?

family members   food   host's hobbies   host's job   location
pets   type of house   type of room available

4 e Read all the texts about the young people and the descriptions of host families. Decide which host family (A–H) would be most suitable for each student (1–5).

1 Sofia ....   3 Sara ....   5 Marco ....
2 Luca ....   4 Daniel ....

5 Find the words in the article which mean these things.

1 free; available (text A) ....
2 meals cooked outside over fire (text B) ....
3 an indoor sport similar to tennis but played with a small object that has feathers on it (text C) ....
4 a meal that you buy at a shop or restaurant and eat at home (text C) ....
5 give something to someone (text E) ....
6 a journey in a vehicle, when you are not driving (text G) ....
7 things made with milk (text H) ....

Sara loves animals and spends a lot of time reading. She uses a wheelchair, so she is unable to use stairs and needs accommodation close to the school. Sara doesn't eat meat.

Daniel loves listening to and writing music. He doesn't mind if he shares a room or has his own, but he wants to be able to walk to school. Animal hair makes him sneeze.

Marco loves painting and drawing. He'd like to be close to his cousin, who is studying for a degree in the city. He'd also like to be in a family with teenage children.

ATC English Language School

Host family accommodation

A Miss Young

I'm retired and live with my cat Molly. I'm a vegetarian and I love baking and spend hours making delicious cakes and biscuits, which I'm happy to share! I live in a quiet, ground floor flat, just a five-minute walk from the school. I have one spare room with one bed.

B Mr and Mrs Hamilton

We live in a house near a park with an outdoor swimming pool and tennis courts. We're about thirty minutes on foot from the school. Our grown-up children no longer live with us but they attend our amazing weekly barbecues. We have one spare room for two students.

C Mrs Brown

I live in a house on the edge of the city with a large garden. I live with my daughter and her dog. We live close to a gym and we both love playing badminton. We usually cook simple British meals. Sometimes we get a takeaway. We have one spare room for two students.

D Mr and Mrs Puri

We live in a house near the local university with our fifteen-year-old son. We can take one student. We love art and have an art studio in our garden. Family meals usually consist of curries and other Indian food. We don't have any pets but our neighbour's cat sometimes visits!

E Mr and Mrs Lewis

We love art and history, which is lucky because we live close to both an art gallery and a museum! We also enjoy cooking and eat a lot of Italian food. We have a flat on the ground floor of a large house and can provide one student with their own room.

F Mr Lee

I'm a keen cook who loves trying out new recipes from around the world. I also play the guitar in a band. I live in a flat on the second floor of a building, a short bus journey from the school. I have two spare bedrooms, each with one bed.

G Mr Harris and Ms French

We live in a house with our two teenage daughters and our dog Billy. We're just a short bus ride away from the school. We're all huge football fans and watch matches whenever we can. We cook traditional British food. We have one room available with two beds.

H Mr and Mrs Stockwell

We live very close to the school and can offer accommodation for two students sharing a room. We love going to concerts and listen to all kinds of music. We're vegan, so we don't eat meat or dairy products, but we grow our own vegetables and cook tasty food!

7 Travellers' tales

GRAMMAR

defining relative clauses

1 Put the words in the correct order to make sentences.

1 is / the / that / bag / I / yesterday / bought / this

....

2 Emma / looking for / flight / a / that / in /stops / is / Paris

....

3 staying / my / with / live / cousins / Canada / who / in /we're

....

4 where / visited / we / Shakespeare / born / was / house / the

....

5 train / leaves / which / at four / that's / the

....

6 is / friend / visiting / a / he / who / on holiday / met / Liam

....

2 Read the sentences. Circle the relative pronoun if it can be left out.

The motorway (which) they used was very busy.

1 We were in a traffic jam **that** lasted five hours.

2 I visited the village **where** my grandparents got married.

3 What's the name of the website **that** I can use to buy a cheap flight?

4 I've got a friend **who** has won a holiday to New York.

5 The teachers are planning a trip **which** the students will love.

6 The man **who** looked at my passport laughed at the photo.

7 The tourists **that** we saw at the check-in desk were very impatient.

8 The girl **that** I met lived in a small village near our hotel.

3 Complete the sentences with *who*, *which* or *where*. If a relative pronoun is not necessary, write '–'.

1 I've got this new rucksack .... is perfect for going camping.

2 Max can't find the photo .... he needs for his passport.

3 I know a boy .... always arrives ten to fifteen minutes late.

4 We went to a restaurant .... you can eat as much as you want for twenty euros.

5 There's a boy in my class .... speaks five different languages.

6 The sightseeing trip .... my dad booked was brilliant.

7 Anna enjoyed the trip .... her friends organised for her birthday.

8 We stayed in a very small town .... everyone knew each other.

4 🔊 7.1 Listen and check your answers.

5 Complete the blog post with *who*, *which*, *where* or *that*. Sometimes more than one answer is possible. If a relative pronoun is not necessary, write '–'.

A big summer at Big Lake Summer Camp

For your holiday this year, try a place **1**........................... you can enjoy something really different. Try Big Lake Summer Camp! I went last year and it was a holiday **2**........................... I will never forget. Each day there are different activities **3**........................... you can choose from an amazing programme. You learn with teachers **4**........................... are experts in their activity. I tried activities **5**........................... were completely new for me, like sky-diving and film-making.

At first, I was very nervous because I didn't know anyone, but I soon found friends **6**........................... were doing the same activities as me. The weekends were more relaxing, with shopping trips and sightseeing in parts of the island **7**........................... not many people go. One day we met some people in the town **8**........................... invited us to their party. It was brilliant!

6 Choose the correct words. Then complete the sentences to make them true for you.

1 A person **which** / **who** I really admire is .... because ....

2 An object **who** / **which** is important to me is .... because ....

3 A family member **that** / **which** I'm close to is .... because

....

4 A place **where** / **which** I spend a lot of time is .... because ....

5 One thing **that** / **who** I always take with me when I travel is .... because ....

VOCABULARY

travel

1 Complete the travel words in the sentences. The first and last letters are given.

1 She didn't enjoy the f _ _ _ t to New York because the plane was hot and noisy.
2 You can't travel to another country if you don't have a p _ _ _ _ _ t.
3 This snow is going to d _ _ _ y the bus and we'll arrive late.
4 The j _ _ _ _ y home took eight hours and it was very long and boring.
5 The planes can't l _ _ d on this island because there are too many mountains.
6 We're going on a t _ _ p to Disneyland. I can't wait!
7 Liam and his friends walked over the b _ _ _ _ r from Austria into Italy.
8 Lee and her family are going to t _ _ _ _ l around Europe by train this summer.

2 🔊 7.2 Listen and match the speakers (1–6) with the photos (A–F).

3 Read the sentences. Decide if the word in bold is a noun (N) or a verb (V).

1 It took us a long time to **check in** our bags because the airport was very busy. ....
2 The students always enjoy going on a **trip** to the theatre. ....
3 I don't think the plane can **land** in this weather. ....
4 I was frightened during the **take-off** because the plane made a loud noise. ....
5 Emily met some friends on the train **journey**. ....
6 One day I want to **travel** around the world. ....
7 After a long **delay** they finally announced our flight. ....
8 Air **travel** is becoming more expensive. ....

4 Complete the conversation with these words.

abroad   flights   journey   motorway   passport
sightseeing   travelling   trip

> Guess what! I'm going on a school ¹............................ to Istanbul in the spring!

> Really? Wow! How are you ²............................ there?

> By coach. The ³............................ are too expensive.

> I bet that's a long way.

> Yeah, thirty-six hours. It'll be a really boring ⁴............................ too. We'll be on the ⁵............................ most of the time.

> Is it your first time ⁶............................?

> Yeah. We usually just go camping around here. I've just got my ⁷............................ out because our teacher wants to see them all.

> How's the photo?!

> So embarrassing. It's four years old. I look so young!

> What are you going to do while you're in Istanbul?

> We're going to visit a school there and, of course, we'll go ⁸............................ to see some of the most interesting places in the city.

Extend

5 🔊 7.3 Listen and match the definitions (1–8) with these words. There are six words you do not need.

boarding card   brochure   charter   cruise   currency
departure   full board   half board   luggage   package   route
self-catering   subway   youth hostel

1	5 ....
2	6 ....
3	7 ....
4	8 ....

6 Write a paragraph describing a holiday or trip you went on. Try to use words from this page.

LISTENING

1 Read the sentences about a YouTube channel. Decide which type of word (A–F) is needed to complete each sentence (1–6).

A an action .... **D** people ....
B a date .... **E** a place ....
C a number .... **F** a thing ....

1 The YouTube channel is about travelling in the south of ....

2 The presenters show you places that you could .... in the future.

3 They talk to .... about their experiences of the area.

4 They teach you about local ....

5 The next episode comes out on ....

6 Each episode is about .... minutes long.

2 🔊 7.4 Listen and complete the sentences in Ex 1.

3 (e) 🔊 7.5 You will hear a boy called Alfie Sanchez talking about an online travel show he presents. Listen and complete the sentences. Write one word or a number or a date or a time.

AN ONLINE TRAVEL SHOW

Alfie started recording his trips when he was
¹... years old.

The first place Alfie filmed was a
Scottish ²... .

Alfie used to travel with his parents
and his ³... .

Alfie chooses his destinations by
reading ⁴... .

Alfie really enjoys learning about
⁵... .

His videos sometimes include an
⁶... with a local person.

---

modals of obligation, prohibition and necessity

4 Match the first sentences (1–6) to the second sentences (A–F).

1 You must get a passport.
2 There's a lot of snow on the road.
3 We don't have to go sightseeing now.
4 They have to go now.
5 Jake will be late because of the traffic jam.
6 You mustn't leave your bag there.

A Somebody might take it.
B We must drive slowly.
C You can't travel abroad without it.
D We need to start without him.
E The train leaves in ten minutes.
F Everything is open tomorrow.

5 Choose the correct answers (A, B or C) to complete the conversation.

A: So, are you ready for your holiday?

B: No, not at all. My passport's only just arrived. I ¹....... get a new one because I lost my old one.

A: That's typical of you! When do you ²....... leave?

B: We're flying at seven o'clock in the morning, so we ³....... be at the airport by five o'clock. Dad says we ⁴....... leave the house early in case there's a traffic jam.

A: But you hate getting up early!

B: I know. I ⁵....... forget to set my alarm. Anyway, I'm going to pack my bags and then I'm going to bed.

A: That's a pity. I'm just going to Anna's party.

B: Anna's party? Hang on, let me think. I ⁶....... pack now.

A: Yes, you do, Maria. You can come to the party, but you ⁷....... pack first. I'll come and help. We ⁸....... be there until nine o'clock.

B: Brilliant! I hate packing, but I'll do it faster if you help me.

1 A 'll need to **B** had to **C** must
2 A have to **B** must **C** will have to
3 A had to **B** don't have to **C** 'll have to
4 A mustn't **B** had to **C** must
5 A don't have to **B** mustn't **C** must
6 A didn't have to **B** don't need to **C** must
7 A had to **B** have to **C** don't have to
8 A mustn't **B** didn't have to **C** don't need to

SPEAKING

1 Match the question halves (1–6) to (A–F) to complete the questions.

1 What kinds of travel problems do
2 Do you prefer to travel
3 What's the best holiday
4 Which is more fun:
5 What do you do if
6 Why do people

A you've ever had?
B people experience on holiday?
C you're bored on holiday?
D going to the beach or going to the mountains?
E go on holiday?
F by plane or by train?

2 🔊 7.6 Listen to two students answering questions from Ex 1. Which two questions do they answer? What answers do they give?

....
....
....
....

3 🔊 7.7 Listen again and complete the extracts from the conversation. Why does the boy use the highlighted phrases?

1 **Mariam:** I've never been on a plane.
   Ben: .... Mariam, I've been on a plane.

2 **Mariam:** I think going to the beach is more fun because there are more things to do there.
   Ben: As Mariam ...., there are lots of things to do at the beach.

Ben uses the highlighted phrases to ....
....

4 Complete the extracts from another conversation with these phrases. You do not need three of the phrases.

---
as Eva said   I agree with Eva
I'm not sure I agree with Eva   I've never done that   like Eva
that's never happened to me   unlike Eva
---

1 **A:** A common problem is that people lose their luggage on their flight. It happened to my grandparents once.
   B: ...., but our flight was delayed last year and we had to sit in the airport for eight hours.

2 **A:** The best holiday I've ever had was at a campsite near a river. I learnt how to fish and then cook the fish on the barbecue.
   B: .... My favourite holiday was to Venice. I loved all the old buildings there. It was really beautiful.

3 **A:** When I'm bored on holiday, I watch a film on my phone or tablet if I can.
   B: ...., I watch a film or I read a book. I usually have some books on my phone.

4 **A:** People go on holiday to relax for a week or two. They want to stop thinking about their work and do something fun.
   B: .... People get very stressed these days, so they need to relax. Holidays help them to do that.

5 🔊 7.8 Listen and check your answers.

6 🔊 7.9 Think about your own holiday experiences. Then listen to the girl's comments again from Ex 3. Record your own responses using the phrase from Ex 3.

7 Listen to your recording from Ex 6. Compare. Check the things you are happy with in your recording.

Stress and intonation ☐
Speed ☐
Pronunciation ☐
Enthusiasm ☐

Record yourself again and try to improve on the ones you weren't happy with.

WRITING

an article

1 Read the advert. What information should you include in your article?

Tips for
travelling around your city or town

Tell us about the different ways of getting around.

Say which is the best.
Say which is the worst.

Write an article describing these three points and we will publish the most interesting ones on our site.

Around 100 words, please!

2 Choose the best opening question for the article in Ex 1.

A Have you ever travelled to school by boat?

B How important is the tram system in your city?

C How many different ways are there to get around where you live?

3 Choose the best closing question / statement for the article in Ex 1.

A Have you got any good suggestions for places to visit?

B What would you recommend to visitors in your town or city?

C Let me know if there are more different types in your area.

4 Complete a student's article with these adjectives.

better   cheaper   popular   second-hand   useful

Top tips for getting around Cambridge

by Louise Bower

How many different ways are there to get around your city? In Cambridge, there's a bus network, a train service and there are plenty of taxis. However, cycling is the most [1]........................... form of transport.

Thousands of people travel around the city by bike every day. It's [2]........................... than other forms of transport and you can avoid the traffic. It's also [3]........................... for your health. You can hire a bike or you can buy a [4]........................... one.

The train is probably the least [5]........................... way to get around because it takes you away from the city, not around it.

So, that's Cambridge. What would you recommend to visitors in your town or city?

5 Read the advert in Ex 1 again and make notes to plan your article. Think about these things.

1 What title will you give your article?

2 Think of an opening question to the reader.

3 Look at your answer to Ex 1 and make notes for each point you need to include.

4 Think of a closing statement or question to the reader.

6 e Write your article in about 100 words. Use your notes from Ex 5.

UNIT CHECK

1 Complete the sentences with relative pronouns. Sometimes more than one answer is possible. If a pronoun is not necessary, write '–'.

1 Do you remember the girl .... sat next to us on the plane?

2 The city .... I want to visit the most is Buenos Aires.

3 We're travelling on the train .... goes to Dublin.

4 The people .... work here are nice and very friendly.

5 Where are the tickets .... I gave you this morning?

6 There was a long delay at the airport .... made people angry.

7 The place .... I love the most is definitely Venice.

8 I love places .... I can have fun.

2 Complete the sentences with these verbs.

didn't have to	don't have to	had to	'll have to
	mustn't	need to	

1 You .... buy the tickets online, but they're cheaper.

2 The train stopped at the border because we .... show our passports.

3 I .... see the doctor. I've had a headache for two days.

4 We .... be late. The bus will leave without us.

5 Alice .... travel on her own. She met an old friend on the train.

6 The flight leaves tomorrow at 6 a.m. We .... get up very early.

3 Put the letters in the correct order to make travel words. Find the hidden message.

n a l d → | l | a | n | d |
                4

1 e a d y l → | d | | | |
                    3

2 d a b o r a → | | | | o | | |
                        10   8

3 n y u r e j o → | | | | | | |
                        6

4 r o t s a p s p → | p | | | | | | |
                            12 7

5 h i e t n g e s g i s → | s | | | | | s | | | | |
                              11 1 9   5

6 s i t n i t e n a d o → | d | | | | | | | | | n |
                                      2

| | | V | | | | | | | | | | | | | | |
 1 2 3 4   5 6 7 8   9 10 11 12

4 Choose the correct answers to complete the sentences.

1 A lot of people are waiting to .... their bags at the airport.
   A delay   B check in   C take off

2 During the two-hour ...., we ate our sandwiches and watched a film.
   A flight   B border   C motorway

3 Oliver heard about the .... in the town centre, so he decided to go by bike.
   A border   B motorway   C traffic jam

4 Today the students are .... in London, but tomorrow they begin their classes.
   A travelling   B abroad   C sightseeing

5 Alice enjoyed her holiday in Brazil, but she's very tired after the long .... home.
   A journey   B time   C travel

6 I'm always very nervous during ...., but once the plane is in the air, I'm fine.
   A delay   B take-off   C check-in

5 Complete the words in the blog post. The first and last letters are given.

A memorable trip

Last year my family and I went on a ¹c_ _ _ _e around the Mediterranean on a huge ship. It was like a city! We took a ²f_ _ _ _t from London to Barcelona and got on the ship there. There were five different ³d_ _ _ _ _ _ _ _ _s over the week, including Naples and Rome. We didn't ⁴h_ _e to get off the ship in each place but, of course, we wanted to do some ⁵s_ _ _ _ _ _ _ _g. We ⁶h_d to be back on the ship by a certain time, though, or we could be left behind. In Rome, we paid a ⁷g_ _ _e to show us around the main sights. It's such a beautiful city! The only problem was the ⁸t_ _ _ _ _c jams on most of the roads, ⁹w_ _ _h made it difficult to get to all the places we wanted to see.

But the best thing about the trip was the food. The holiday was ¹⁰full-b_ _ _d, so there was food to eat all day. And eat we did!

READING

1 Complete the article with these words.

continuously   decreasing   development   improve   increase   progress

Smartphones
aren't **all** bad news!

We hear a lot of bad things in the news about smartphones and the way they are changing our world. But let's stop for a minute and think about all the ways they help us make **1**............................. .

Smartphones keep us safe. Those apps which **2**........................... track our location help our friends and family know where we are all the time. And they can even help the emergency services to find people who are trapped after disasters such as earthquakes.

Smartphones actually **3**...........................our brains – we don't need to remember lots of facts any more because we can look them up on the internet. But this doesn't mean our brain power is **4**........................... – it's just that we have learned how to find information quickly and then we organise it differently in our brains.

Smartphones are also helping the **5**........................... of poorer countries. If you think about it, buying a few smartphones or tablets gives a school access to all the information on the internet. How many textbooks would they need to buy to get the same amount of knowledge?

Finally, smartphones **6**........................... our free time. Being able to shop, check emails and find information on our phones saves time. One study claims we have twenty-two extra days of free time a year, all thanks to our phones!

2 Read the article about taking photos quickly. What experience is the writer describing? Does she feel this was generally a good or bad experience?

....

....

3 **e** Read the article again and choose the correct answer (A, B, C or D).

1 In the writer's opinion, the best thing about smartphone photos is that they are

  A very good quality.   **C** instant.

  B inexpensive.   **D** easy to post online.

2 The writer began the project in order to

  A remember what she did for a year.

  B share her experiences with people she knows.

  C improve her photography skills.

  D make a decision about her education.

3 In the third paragraph, the writer says that selecting the right images for her project was sometimes

  A relaxing.   **C** difficult.

  B boring.   **D** impossible.

4 At the end of the project, the writer felt

  A worried that she hadn't achieved her aim.

  B sad that she couldn't continue working on it.

  C happy that she had so many good memories.

  D surprised by how much she enjoyed it.

5 What would be a good introduction to this article?

  A Photography student Helen Winter writes about how to take better photos with your smartphone.

  B Helen Winter describes how she created a daily picture diary.

  C Do we use our camera phones too much? Student Helen Winter discusses this question.

  D Helen Winter, 16, argues that we can make art with everyday photographs.

4 Find words or phrases in the article that have these meanings.

1 photos (para 1) ....

2 a lot of money (para 1) ....

3 record an event, activity, etc. in a photo or on video (para 1) ....

4 remember something from the past (para 2) ....

5 be an expert in a subject (para 2) ....

6 worrying (para 3) ....

I took a photo a day for a whole year! by Helen Winter

Like most young people nowadays, I love taking photos with my smartphone. Even before I started the '365 Photos' project, I took lots of snaps of my family, my pets and sometimes even my dinner! I love the fact that without spending a fortune, you can take excellent photos with a smartphone, which you can then share on social media – something I also really enjoy doing! But most of all I love the way that you can photograph something at the exact moment you see it. You can capture a moment in time.

When one of my friends told me that she had started the project, I thought it was a great idea. I wanted to use the photos to create a record of the year for me to look back on. But what I didn't realise at the start was that it would also make me a better photographer. Now I even want to specialise in photography at art school.

I thought that taking a picture every day would be simple, and on some days it was – in fact, it was hard to choose just one picture as there were so many I liked. But on other days all the photos seemed uninteresting and it was quite stressful to find one that was good enough to keep. It was only when I looked back on the whole year that I saw that some of the simplest shots were the most meaningful.

When I finally had my 365 photos, I couldn't believe it had been a whole year. At the beginning it felt like it would be a very long time but actually, it was over before I knew it – time went by really quickly. You would think that I would be glad to have a year of experiences captured on camera, but mostly I felt sorry it was over. I knew I was going to miss it. But looking at all my photos also made me realise that you don't have to be a really creative person to make art. All it takes is some happy moments – and a smartphone!

5 Complete the sentences with words from Ex 4 in the correct form.

1 We will .... these days as a special time when we're older.

2 This is a very .... time for her – she's studying for her end-of-year exams.

3 Dave spent .... on his new phone – it cost around 1,000 euros!

4 I love this .... of my basketball team. Look how happy we all look.

5 Wait, let me take a photo. I want to .... this happy moment!

6 I want to .... in Russian history in college. I find it fascinating!

GRAMMAR

reported speech

1 Complete the reported statements with pronouns.

1 'I love making paper planes for my little brother.'

Nathan said that .... loved making paper planes for .... little brother.

2 'We aren't going to your party, Kate.'

We told Kate that .... weren't going to .... party.

3 'We often take photos of our friends.'

They said that .... often took photos of .... friends.

4 'I'm making a film for my school project.'

Anna said that .... was making a film for .... school project.

5 'I can't find the information you need.'

Olivia told me that .... couldn't find the information .... needed.

2 Complete the conversation with the correct form of the verbs in brackets.

A: Are you coming to drama class tonight?

B: No, I can't. I told my parents I **1**........................... (will) look after my little brother tonight.

A: But Dan, the drama teacher said we **2**........................... (have to) be at the last class. She said we **3**........................... (need) to practise the songs.

B: I know, but my parents are working. I told them it **4**........................... (be) my last drama class, but they said they **5**........................... (not want) Tom to be on his own.

A: Wait a minute. I can help. My brother said he **6**........................... (want) to watch basketball on TV tonight. Perhaps you could leave Tom at my house with him?

B: That's a great idea. Tom told me they **7**........................... (like) the same team.

A: See? I said that I **8**........................... (can) help!

3 Read the conversations below. Then complete Maria's diary entry at the top of the page with the things they said.

Monday

Music teacher

Maria plays the guitar really well.

That's great! Her mum and I can't play any instruments. I'll get her a new guitar.

Dad

Tuesday

Me

I can help to pay for the guitar.

Don't worry, Grandad's going to pay for it. He wants to help. And he loves guitar music.

Dad

Monday

Mum and Dad have just got back from parents' evening at school. My music teacher told Dad that I **1**............................... the guitar really well. Dad said that he **2**............................... really surprised because he and Mum **3**............................... any instruments. Then Dad said that he **4**............................... me a new guitar. Brilliant!

Tuesday

I told Dad that I **5**............................... to pay for the guitar, but he said that Grandad **6**............................... for it and that he **7**............................... to help. Dad also said Grandad **8**............................... guitar music. Well, he'll be my first fan! I'll play for him when I'm good enough!

4 8.1 Read the reported questions and write the direct speech. Listen and check your answers.

1 She asked me if she was in the right queue for tickets.

'...?'

2 He asked a girl where he could buy a souvenir.

'...?'

3 Ian asked his friend what day it was.

'...?'

4 Her mum asked her if she needed her swimming costume.

'...?'

5 Martha asked me when my friend was going to arrive.

'...?'

6 I asked them if their parents were going to pick them up after the match.

'...?'

7 The teacher asked him where his sister was.

'...?'

8 The boy asked his friend if she had a phone charger.

'...?'

5 Rewrite the statements and questions in reported speech.

1 'I'll send you the photos.'

Harry told me that ....

2 'You can leave.'

Emma told her friends that ....

3 'I'm tired.'

Dan said that ....

4 'Can you read us your story again?'

They asked me ....

5 'Our photos aren't very good.'

They said that ....

6 'What time can I call you?'

Alice asked me ....

VOCABULARY

hobbies and interests

1 Match the words (1–7) with the hobbies and interests (A–G).

1 taking		**A**	a musical instrument
2 doing		**B**	jewellery
3 keeping		**C**	fit
4 making		**D**	gaming
5 online		**E**	drama
6 practising		**F**	figures
7 collecting action		**G**	photos

2 🔊 8.2 Listen to six people talking about their hobbies. What are they? Whose hobby is not mentioned in Ex 1?

1 Maria: ....
2 Amy: ....
3 Max: ....
4 Daniel: ....
5 Fred: ....
6 Katie: ....

..........................'s hobby is not mentioned in Ex 1.

3 Complete the sentences with these words.

---

battery   glue   ingredients   lens   paintbrush   recipe

---

1 The problem with my new camera is the .... It doesn't last long.

2 Jack's got an art exam tomorrow, so he's gone to buy a new ....

3 I've broken a cup. Maybe I can repair it with some ....

4 Amelia bought the .... for a chocolate cake, but she forgot the flour.

5 I used the zoom .... for this photo – that's why you can see all the details.

6 I downloaded a .... for pancakes. Shall we make some?

4 Choose the correct words to complete the email.

Hi Kieran,

How was your weekend? Did you chill **1**in / out all weekend?

My cousin arrived on Friday evening and we went to the beach. She is mad **2**about / with taking photos, and she took some at sunset.

On Saturday we stayed in and **3**did / made some really cool 3D models of animals. My little sister wanted to join **4**in / out, but she was really annoying!

Yesterday it was sunny and we went to the new skateboarding park – I **5**go / am into skateboarding at the moment! The park is a great place to hang **6**over / out and I've made lots of friends. Shall we go together?

Bye for now,

Laura

Extend

5 Match sentences (1–5) with the descriptions (A–E).

1 Robert is usually smiling. ....
2 Nick is a very good musician. ....
3 Gary always tells the truth. ....
4 Ted wouldn't hurt anybody. ....
5 Oliver makes really funny jokes. ....

A He's honest.
B He's got a good sense of humour.
C He's kind.
D He's cheerful.
E He's talented.

6 Complete the conversation with words and phrases from Ex 5.

A: You look very **1**.......................... ! Good news?

B: Yes! I won that competition … First prize! Can you believe it?

A: Wow … Congratulations! I'm not really surprised, though – you are so **2**.......................... .

B: You are very **3**.......................... . But to be **4**.........................., there were so many other people who made creative things!

A: Have you told your mum yet?

B: Not yet … maybe I should pretend I didn't win and then surprise her with the news!

A: That's so mean. You have a very strange **5**.......................... .

7 Choose the correct words to complete the sentences about getting better at things.

1 The other team **defeated** / **checked** us on Saturday. We couldn't win!

2 She has already **got on** / **achieved** a lot in her life by the age of 18.

3 John is confident that he can **take** / **lead** the group to success.

4 Tomorrow Mr Brown will **attempt** / **plan** to do that crazy experiment!

5 If you don't try, you can never **attempt** / **succeed**.

LISTENING

1 🔊 **8.3 Listen and choose the number or date you hear.**

1	**A**	13/05/2006	**B**	30/05/2006	**C**	30/05/2016
2	**A**	€10.99	**B**	€99.10	**C**	€10.09
3	**A**	5,050	**B**	5,005	**C**	5,500
4	**A**	80%	**B**	18%	**C**	8%
5	**A**	2.75	**B**	275	**C**	2,750
6	**A**	12/12/1972	**B**	2/12/1972	**C**	22/12/1927
7	**A**	419	**B**	490	**C**	4,019
8	**A**	30.2%	**B**	13.2%	**C**	13.02%

2 Record yourself reading your answers to Ex 1. Then listen again to track 8.3 and compare.

3 🇪 🔊 **8.4 Listen. Then choose the correct answer for each question.**

1 Which ingredient does the girl need to buy?

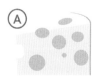 

2 What is the boy's hobby?

3 What does the girl need to buy after school?

4 Which photo did the girl take at the weekend?

5 Which instrument does the boy want to learn?

6 Where does the girl want to meet Jack on Saturday?

7 What's the boy most looking forward to this weekend?

indirect questions

4 Find and correct the mistakes in five of the indirect questions.

1 Do you know if do they serve vegetarian food here?

....

2 Can you say me why you like collecting action figures?

....

3 Can I ask you where you usually go to practise windsurfing?

....

4 Do you know how many goals did the team score?

....

5 Do you know if she's going to take the photography course?

....

6 Can you tell me what do I have to do?

....

7 Can I ask you if you have tried online gaming?

....

8 Do you know if did they win the match?

....

5 Read what the people asked and complete the indirect questions below.

1 Why is the plane late?
2 What time does the film finish?
3 Is this the right battery for my phone?
4 Where did you take this photo?
5 Are they coming to practise with us?
6 Did you edit this video?
7 How long does the cooking course last?
8 Have you seen my guitar?

1 Do you know .... ?
2 Can you tell me .... ?
3 Do you know .... ?
4 Can I ask you .... ?
5 Do you know .... ?
6 Can you tell me .... ?
7 Do you know .... ?
8 Can I ask .... ?

SPEAKING

1 🔊 8.5 Listen and decide if the speakers are making a suggestion (M) or responding to a suggestion (R).

1	3	5	7 ....
2	4	6	8 ....

2 🔊 8.6 Choose the correct words to complete the conversation. Then listen and check your answers.

A: OK, so we need to finish building this today and we only have two hours. **¹Why don't we / How about** asking Ryan and Emma to help?

B: I'm not **²sure / agreed** about that. I'd rather we worked it out ourselves.

A: OK. **³What about / Why don't we** look in the manual again and go back through each step in the instructions?

B: **⁴You've / That's** a great idea. Then we can see if we have missed anything.

A: **⁵Shall / Would** I check we've got all the pieces while you read aloud?

B: **⁶Agreeing / Agreed**. I'll read and you check. And I'll tick each instruction as we check it.

A: Yes, OK. This all sounds **⁷as / like** a good idea. **⁸Let's / Shall** we see if it works!

3 Read the speaking task in the box below and answer the questions.

1 Who are you going to talk about?
2 When is this person going to do the course?
3 What does this person want to learn?
4 How many courses do you need to choose?

> A girl in your class wants to learn a new skill over the summer holidays. Here are some of the things she could study on a short course. Talk together about the different courses and say which one you think would be the best.

4 🔊 8.7 Listen to two students discussing the courses. Which course do they NOT talk about? Which course do they choose?

5 🔊 8.8 Match the suggestions (1–5) with the reasons (A–E). Listen again and check your answers.

1 How about the computer course? ....
2 What about learning chess? ....
3 How about learning the guitar? ....
4 Why don't we recommend something more creative, then? ....
5 So maybe the writing course? ....

A Playing matches would be fun.

B Painting is creative, but I think it's for older people.

C It's interesting, creative and it could also help her with her school work.

D Yes, a musical instrument is a nice idea, but she may prefer something she can make progress in.

E I think it would be interesting to know how to program a computer.

6 🔊 8.9 Listen to another student's suggestions for the speaking task. Follow the instructions to respond, using the words in brackets. Record yourself.

1 Accept the suggestion: creative and useful (*great idea*)
2 Reject the suggestion: a fun / creative activity = better for summer holidays (*nice idea, but*)
3 Reject the suggestion: a bit boring; choose something more exciting (*sounds, prefer*)
4 Accept the suggestion: creative, relaxing and fun (*sounds*)
5 Reject the suggestion: very expensive (*not sure*)

7 🔊 8.10 Listen to your recording from Ex 6. Then listen to another student's responses on track 8.10. Compare.

Summer holiday activities

71

WRITING

an article

1 How would you describe these hobbies? Write them in the correct column for you.

3D printing   coding   kickboxing   making comics
playing the piano   skateboarding

creative	exciting	unusual

2 Read the advert below and answer the questions.

1 Who is the message for?

....

2 What do they need to write?

....

3 How many words should they write?

....

4 How many questions do they need to answer?

....

Articles wanted!

We'd like to know more about you, the members of our school sports teams!

Send us a short article about your favourite hobby (except sports, of course!). How and why did you start doing it? When and where do you do it? Why do you enjoy it?

We'll post your article as part of your online profile on the school website. Only about 100 words, please!

3 Read a student's article and complete it with these words.

amazing   exciting   really   relaxing   surprised   unusual

My surprising hobby
by Sam Goodyear

You might be ¹........................... to know that my hobby is singing in a choir! It's quite ²........................... for footballers to sing in public, but I saw the choir performing one day and they were ³........................... ! I decided I wanted to join. At first I was ⁴........................... nervous, but now I've been in the choir for a year and I love it.

We meet every Friday to rehearse. We sing all kinds of music and prepare for concerts. We sometimes sing in public places like shopping centres or in the street.

Being in a choir helps me forget about my worries – it's very ⁵........................... . I also find singing in concerts very ⁶........................... . There are lots of people watching – just like a football match!

4 Think of a hobby you do regularly. Choose the reasons why you like it. Can you think of any more? Add them to the list.

- It's fun. ☐
- It's really interesting. ☐
- It helps me to keep fit. ☐
- It's a good way to socialise. ☐
- It's very creative. ☐
- It's relaxing. ☐
- ....
- ....

5 Read the advert in Ex 2 again. Imagine you are a member of a sports team at your school and want to send in your article. Make notes to plan your answer.

my hobby: ....

how I started and why:

....
....

when and where I do it:

....
....

why I like it:

....
....

6 Write your article in about 100 words. Use your notes from Ex 5 to help you.

UNIT CHECK

1 Rewrite the statements in reported speech. Use the reporting verb in brackets.

1 Luke: 'The cake is delicious.' (say)

....

....

2 Me to Amy: 'I'll email you the photos.' (tell)

....

....

3 Rachel and Ian: 'We're bored.' (say)

....

....

4 Grandma and Grandpa: 'We'll be at the beach at ten o'clock.' (say)

....

....

5 Neil to me: 'I love keeping fit.' (tell)

....

....

6 Emma to her sister: 'You can't use my camera.' (tell)

....

....

2 Nick is interviewing Amanda Forrester, a famous skier. Report his questions.

1 Are you practising for a competition?
2 Where do you train?
3 Do you sometimes fall over?
4 How do you feel before a competition?
5 Are you going to take part in the local tournament this year?
6 Are your parents here to watch you?

1 ....

....

2 ....

....

3 ....

....

4 ....

....

5 ....

....

6 ....

....

3 Complete the interview with Jo, a teenage fashion designer. Use the questions in brackets to make indirect questions.

Hi, Jo. I love your dress! Can I ask you ¹...? (Did you make it?)

Yes, I did. I made it for a friend's party.

Can you tell us ²...? (How long does it take to design a dress?)

It depends. Sometimes a day, sometimes weeks.

Could I ask you ³...? (When did you start designing?)

When I was twelve!

Wow! And do you know ⁴...? (Are there many professional teenage designers?)

Yes, there are. And some of them are very good.

Can you tell us ⁵...? (What do you want to do in the future?)

Yes, I'd love to run my own business.

And finally, can I ask you ⁶...? (Have you ever made a dress for a famous person?)

No, I haven't, but I'd like to one day.

4 Look at the photos and write the hobbies and interests.

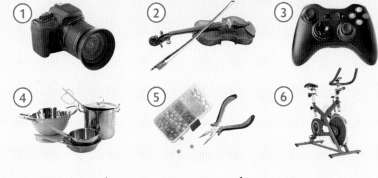

1 .... photos
2 .... instrument
3 online ....
4 ....
5 making ....
6 .... fit

5 Match (1–6) with (A–F) to complete the descriptions.

1 My dad is mad about cooking. He
2 Those are my sister's paintbrushes. She
3 He's making a model. He
4 I can't take photos because my phone
5 She's really into photography. Her camera
6 We've got all the ingredients so we

A is using special glue.
B has got an amazing zoom lens.
C can start cooking.
D loves trying new recipes.
E is doing an art course.
F has no battery.

9 Life experiences

READING

1 Complete the advert with these words.

---
classic   loads   original   proud   put together   remind

A **holiday** with a **difference**!

Are you looking for somewhere unique and
¹............................ to stay this summer? We have
²............................ a selection of places to stay which
are truly amazing – like this tree house in the Brecon
Beacons. The tree house has ³............................ of modern
features, such as a hot tub and wi-fi, combined with the
⁴............................ things you expect from a tree house:
an artistic structure made from natural
materials and amazing views.
And what could be better than
waking up in the branches of a
tree to ⁵............................ you of
the beauty of the forest?

We are very ⁶............................
of our new collection and look
forward to welcoming you soon.
Book online now!

2 Read the blog post about New York and answer the questions.

1 Why was this trip a new experience for Anna and her family?

....

2 Where do Anna and her family live?

....

3 What kind of pet do they have?

....

4 How did Anna feel at first about someone sleeping in her room?

....

5 Which sport did the family watch in New York?

....

6 Does Anna want to have a similar holiday again?

....

3 🄴 Read the blog post again. Five sentences have been removed. Complete the blog post with sentences A–H. There are three extra sentences which you do not need to use.

A First of all, I had a picnic in Central Park.

B Then we got a taxi to the airport.

C They are an American family with two children.

D It wasn't as good as I expected.

E They said they hoped we had enjoyed our stay in New York.

F Then we waited to see who would reply.

G But reading all those instructions, I started to feel a bit worried.

H We were having an amazing time and wanted to stay there forever.

4 Find words and phrases in the blog post that have these meanings.

1 exchanged (para 1) ....

2 contacted (para 3) ....

3 a guide to how something works (para 4)

4 be successful (para 4) ....

5 strange (para 4) ....

6 important and useful to spend time on (para 5) ....

7 passed; was over (para 6) ....

8 something amazing that you will remember forever (para 6) ....

5 Complete the sentences with words from Ex 4 in the correct form.

1 Did your cousin .... with you about coming to stay over the summer?

2 The plans for the journey .... very well. We arrived just before lunch.

3 It's .... to do some research before you visit a new city, so you don't waste time.

4 I .... email addresses with the boys I met on holiday. We're going to write to each other.

5 Time always .... very quickly when you're having a good time, doesn't it?

6 Camping in your garden may seem ...., but actually lots of people do it.

7 Seeing the Taj Mahal was .... for me. Just incredible!

8 If you don't know how it works, we'd better find the ....

My week in
NEW YORK

We've just arrived home and I'm really tired from the flight, but I have to share my experience with you all. This trip was different from any holiday we've been on before because we took part in a house swap. Yes, we actually swapped apartments with another family!

A couple of months ago my parents signed up to a house swap website and advertised our apartment. First, they had to post photos and give lots of information about exactly where we live and what we could offer a family who wanted to visit London. **1**...........................

Luckily, the Baker family got in touch with us. **2**........................... We were really happy to find out that they lived in New York because it was one of the places we had hoped to visit.

Before we left, my brother and I tidied our rooms, cleared some space in our wardrobes and helped Mum and Dad get the rest of the house ready. We also had to write a 'home manual' explaining how to use everything and even how to look after our cat, Barney! **3**........................... I wondered if it was all going to work out. Also, it was a bit worrying to think that someone else would be sleeping in my room. But by the time the holidays started, I had emailed the girl in the American family a few times, and it felt less weird.

When we arrived in New York, we felt like all the preparations had been worthwhile because the apartment we stayed in was fantastic. The Baker family had filled the fridge with food for us and also recommended what to see and do during our stay. I did so many things I've always dreamed of. **4**........................... I also saw the New York skyline from the top of the Rockefeller building. And we watched a live baseball game, which was really exciting.

The week went by very quickly. When we got back, the Baker family had left us a note saying what a great week they'd had in London. **5**........................... It really was the experience of a lifetime, and I hope we'll do another house swap soon. But now I really need to get some sleep!

Night everyone!

Anna

GRAMMAR

past perfect

1 🔊 9.1 Complete the sentences with the past perfect form of the verbs in brackets. Listen to an American girl talk about her house swap experience and check your answers.

1 Ellie was nervous because she .... (never / fly) to another country before.

2 She .... (only / be) on vacation in the US.

3 Their passports .... (just / arrive) in time for the trip.

4 Anna's parents .... (never / drive) on the left before.

5 Ellie .... (not think) that crossing the street would be different.

6 She .... (never / see) a real palace.

2 Read the short story in the sentences (1–8). Choose the action (in bold) that happens first in each sentence.

1 Alex and his friends **decided** to go to the beach after they **had finished studying**.

2 It **had been** warm all day, but it was very windy when they **arrived**.

3 They **sat** on the sand and **ate** the picnic that they **had prepared**.

4 They **went** into the sea, but **hadn't noticed** the red flag warning of danger.

5 Other swimmers **had left** the water, but Alex and Nathan **jumped** into the waves.

6 It **was** difficult to swim because the sea **had become** so wild.

7 Fortunately, a lifeguard **had seen** them and he **called** to them to leave the water.

8 When they **got out** of the water to their bags, everybody else **had left** the beach.

3 Choose the correct verb form to complete the sentences.

1 When I **met / had met** my best friend, he had already been at our school for ages.

2 By the time the girls found their seats, the show **began / had begun**.

3 After the party had finished, they **tidied / had tidied** the house from top to bottom.

4 We **just left / had just left** a message for Anna when she arrived.

5 I **waited / had waited** an hour for the bus when it finally came.

6 He **didn't do / hadn't done** the class because he had left his guitar at home.

7 When she answered the phone, her mum said she **tried / had tried** to call her four times.

8 I **brought / had brought** food to cook dinner, but everyone had already eaten.

4 Complete the blog post with the past perfect or past simple form of the verbs in brackets.

An artistic summer

Last summer I stayed with my aunt – she ¹........................... (invite) me to spend the school holidays with her. She ²........................... (just / open) a summer school for young artists and asked me to help. I'd always got on well with her so I ³........................... (want) to go. The classes had just started when I ⁴........................... (arrive). Most of the students were between fourteen and eighteen and some of them ⁵........................... (already / win) prizes for their art at school. Each day I ⁶........................... (help) my aunt with the activities that she ⁷........................... (plan). One day, I took a group of students to a park to see a brilliant exhibition of huge sculptures. Before I stayed with my aunt I ⁸........................... (not think) much about art. Now I can't wait to be one of her students!

5 Join the sentences. Use the past perfect, the past simple and the words in brackets in each sentence. The first sentence in each pair is the action that happened first.

1 Sam finished his breakfast. His friends arrived. (after)

....

2 She listened to my message. She called me. (when)

....

3 Nick had a few lessons. He began to cook for his friends. (once)

....

4 They always lived in an apartment. They bought the house. (until)

....

5 The gate closed. Hector and his family arrived. (just, when)

....

6 The sun came up. We got to the top of the mountain. (by the time)

....

VOCABULARY

feelings

1 🔊 9.2 How do they feel? Listen and match the speakers (1–6) with the adjectives (A–F).

A confident ....
B guilty ....
C calm ....
D nervous ....
E jealous ....
F disappointed ....

2 Choose the correct words to complete the sentences.

1 It's **worried / worrying** that we haven't heard from Noah yet.
2 I'm **bored / boring** with this game. Let's play something else.
3 There's no mobile phone signal here. It's really **annoyed / annoying**.
4 There's no need to feel **embarrassed / embarrassing**. I understand how you feel.
5 It helps to listen to **relaxed / relaxing** music before an exam.
6 You look **worried / worrying**. Is everything OK?
7 I'm **annoyed / annoying** that you didn't tell me you weren't coming.

3 Read the clues and complete the crossword with *-ed* or *-ing* adjectives.

```
1            2
a            i
3
e
4
b
5
s
              6
              a
```

Across

1 It's .... what you can do when you try!
3 I'm so .... about the concert. I can't wait!
5 The news about Oscar winning a prize was really .... I didn't know he played chess so well.
6 I'm really .... with Tom – he's so late that we've missed the bus.

Down

2 The programme about positive thinking was very .... I couldn't stop watching.
4 That blog's really .... – there's nothing new in it.

4 Complete the blog post with these words.

amazing   annoying   boring   disappointed   embarrassed
exciting   surprised   worried

My first 'glamping' experience

Last weekend was my first time 'glamping' – it's camping but with glamour! It was very near the beach and it was beautiful. There was a(n) ¹........................... tent waiting for us, ready to sleep in. It even had heating! I am usually ²........................... about going to the bathroom when I go camping, but this place had luxury bathrooms with hot showers!

We bought food from the campsite shop and cooked it on our own stove. When it was time to go to sleep, I was ³........................... at how comfortable it all was. It was just like my bed at home. And the ⁴........................... noise from other campers which usually keeps you awake at night? I didn't hear any! I slept really well.

The only problem was that I found the weekend a bit ⁵........................... . We didn't have anything to do because everything was done for us. The things that make camping ⁶........................... , like going exploring, looking for firewood, just didn't happen. I'm ⁷........................... to admit it, but I think that I prefer regular camping after all!

If you like more luxury than you get with normal camping, you should definitely try glamping – you won't be ⁸........................... .

Extend

5 Match adjectives (1–6) with adjectives (A–F) that have similar meanings.

1 nervous
2 frightened
3 annoyed
4 very sad
5 confident
6 guilty

A angry
B positive
C miserable
D ashamed
E anxious
F afraid

6 Complete the sentences to make them true for you.

1 The last time I felt angry was ....
2 I sometimes get anxious ....
3 The most positive person I know is ....
4 I would feel miserable if ....
5 I once felt ashamed when ....

LISTENING

1 🔊 **9.3 Complete the conversation with these words. Listen and check your answers.**

can   don't   ought   shall   should   wouldn't

A: I think I'm ready for the hiking trip. Are you?

B: No, I haven't finished packing yet. What do you think I ¹.......................... take?

A: Well, Mr Blackburn said that we ²..........................
to wear shorts and boots, but also take a hat and sunglasses with us. It ³.......................... be cloudy in the mountains, but it will still be hot.

B: OK. ⁴.......................... I take my guidebook so we won't get lost when we are out walking?

A: I ⁵.......................... if I were you. Remember, we've got to carry everything and that book is really heavy! I think they'll give us maps of the area when we get there.

B: Why ⁶.......................... you take the compass you got for your birthday, then? We can practise orienteering.

A: Good idea.

2 **Read the questions (1–6) in Ex 3 and think about what you need to listen for: feelings (F) or opinions (O)?**

1 ....   3 ....   5 ....
2 ....   4 ....   6 ....

3 🅴 🔊 **9.4 Now listen to the six conversations. For each question, choose the correct answer (A, B or C). Think about your answers to Ex 2.**

1 You will hear two friends talking about an exchange programme. What does the girl think the boy should do?

   A ask his teacher about it

   B talk to his family about it

   C sign up for it

2 You will hear a boy telling a friend about a course he did. How did he feel at the end of the course?

   A embarrassed

   B very tired

   C proud of himself

3 You will hear a girl talking to her brother about a problem she is having with a friend. What does her brother advise her to do?

   A avoid talking about what causes the problem

   B ask her teacher for help

   C ignore what her friend is saying

4 You will hear two friends talking about an event they attended. What do they agree about it?

   A They didn't pack the right things.

   B The music was the most important thing.

   C It wasn't a good idea to go.

5 You will hear a boy talking to a friend about doing chores at home. What do they both think?

   A They don't have time to do everything.

   B Young people shouldn't have to help at home.

   C They need to be more organised.

6 You will hear two friends talking about a football match. How does the boy feel about it?

   A worried

   B confident

   C bored

used to

4 **Complete the sentences. Use the correct form of *used to* and the verbs in brackets.**

1 We .... (enjoy) playing board games.

2 .... (Max / be) in the hiking club?

3 They .... (not like) playing hockey.

4 Jess .... (write) short stories at primary school.

5 I .... (not wear) earrings, but now I do.

6 .... (they / live) next to you?

7 Where .... (you / go) to dance classes?

5 **Complete the interview with a young musician. Use the correct form of *used to* and the verbs in brackets.**

A: Hi, Alice, and well done! I really enjoyed your first solo show. Tell us, ¹.......................... (you / perform) when you were little?

B: Yes, I did. I ².......................... (sing) with my grandparents almost every weekend. They were in a band and they ³.......................... (invite) me to sing with them on stage.

A: So, did they give you singing lessons, too?

B: No, they ⁴.......................... (not have) enough time to give me proper lessons, but I watched and listened and that's how I learned.

A: ⁵.......................... (you / dream) of becoming a famous singer?

B: Not at all! I ⁶.......................... (want) to be a vet!

A: A vet?

B: Yes, I've always loved animals and everybody ⁷.......................... (tell) me I would be a great vet. But now I'm into singing, I just can't stop!

SPEAKING

1 🔊 9.5 Read the speaking task below. Listen to two students discussing the activities. Which activity do they choose? Why?

A group of four friends want to try a new activity at the weekend. Here are some things they could do. Talk together about the different activities, and say which one would be the best.

Weekend activities

2 🔊 9.6 Complete the sentences from the students' discussion with one word in each gap. Listen again and check your answers.

1 What do you .... about playing in a band?
2 How .... a virtual reality game? It would be exciting.
3 Maybe they .... prefer to do something outdoors.
4 Yes, hiking .... good, but I don't think it will be a new activity for all of them.
5 I'm not .... about that. It's quite expensive, isn't it?
6 Yes, you're right. Well, they .... try judo.

3 🔊 9.7 Read the discussion questions below. Listen and match the students (1–6) with the questions they are answering (A–F).

A Which is better: doing sport in a team or doing sport on your own? ....
B Which sport or activity is your favourite? Why? ....
C Would you like to try a dangerous activity, like bungee jumping? ....
D How often do you do sport? ....
E How do you feel about competitive sports? ....
F Do you like trying new things? ....

4 🔊 9.8 Listen again. Which phrases do the students use to talk about their likes and dislikes?

1 I'm into … ☐
2 I'm not into … ☐
3 I'm keen on … ☐
4 I'm not very keen on … ☐
5 I love … ☐
6 I've always loved … ☐
7 I don't like … very much. ☐
8 I quite like … ☐
9 I hate … ☐
10 I can't stand … ☐

5 Put the phrases from Ex 4 in the correct place in the table.

like very much	like	dislike	dislike very much

6 Follow the instructions. Use the words in brackets in your answers. Record yourself.

1 Say that you like team sports very much. (into)
2 Say that you generally like doing indoor sports. (prefer)
3 Say that you really like learning new skills. (absolutely)
4 Say that you hate doing the same thing every weekend. (stand)
5 Say that you don't really like water sports. (keen)
6 Say that you want to do a bungee jump one day. (like)

7 🔊 9.9 Listen to your recording from Ex 6. Then listen to a student saying the same sentences on track 9.9. Compare.

WRITING

a story

1 Read the story below quickly. Which of these sentences starts the story?

A Jo couldn't decide what to do on her birthday.

B Last year Jo had the best birthday ever.

C Jo's birthday wasn't what she had expected.

D Jo wanted to have a birthday party.

A She had invited some friends to go walking in the countryside to celebrate her birthday. The weather was sunny. ¹First / Next, they walked up a large hill. They were chatting and enjoying the day.

B ²In the end / After a while, Jo noticed some black clouds in the sky, so they all ran down the hill. ³Finally / Suddenly, Jo's friend Ellen fell over and hurt her ankle. The girls panicked for a while. ⁴After / Then they had calmed down, Jo asked two girls to go back down the hill to get help.

C ⁵Eventually / Suddenly, one of the parents arrived with some paramedics, who helped Ellen. ⁶After / Finally, they went back to Jo's house, got dry and had some birthday cake. They were happy that their friend was safe.

2 Read the story in Ex 1 again and choose the correct words to complete it.

3 Read the story in Ex 1 again. In which paragraph does the writer talk about these things?

1 what Jo did about the situation ....
2 what surprising thing happened ....
3 the reason for the trip ....
4 what happened in the end ....
5 how everyone reacted at first ....
6 how the girls felt at the end ....

4 Read the exam task and two students' notes below (A and B). For each set of notes, decide where the points should go in the story: at the beginning (B), middle (M) or end (E)? Choose two points for each part.

> Your English teacher has asked you to write a story.
> Your story must begin with this sentence:
>
> Eric would never forget his trip to the mountains.
>
> Write your **story** in about **100 words**.

Ⓐ

1 Eric gets a prize for helping the eagles. ☐
2 Eric walks up a mountain to take pictures. ☐
3 Eric takes photos of a man who is stealing eggs. ☐
4 Eric phones a wildlife organization and tells them about the man. ☐
5 Eric has got a new camera he wants to try. ☐
6 Eric finds a very rare eagle's nest. ☐

Ⓑ

1 Eric and his friends get lost. ....
2 Eric and his friends decide to go hiking. ....
3 Eric and his friends realise they have forgotten to take a map or satnav. ....
4 Eric takes a heavy rucksack with lots of food and drink. ....
5 Eric and his friends build a fire to make a signal. ....
6 A mountain rescue team finds Eric and his friends. ....

5 Write a story for the writing task in Ex 4. Use the plans in Ex 4 or your own ideas. Write about 100 words and try to use a range of words and phrases to order the events in the story.

UNIT CHECK

1 Complete the sentences with the past perfect form of the verb in brackets.

1 I .... (not swim) in the sea until I went to Mallorca.
2 The lesson .... (just / start) when we arrived.
3 We .... (not write) a shopping list before we went to the market.
4 My dad came to meet me after he .... (finish) work.
5 Their train .... (already / leave), so we couldn't wave 'goodbye'.
6 Until she saw the audience, she .... (not feel) nervous.

2 Complete the text with the past perfect or past simple form of the verbs in brackets.

When I got home yesterday mum **1**........................ (be) very stressed. The oven **2**........................ (break) and she **3**........................ (invite) friends around for dinner. I **4**........................ (say) I would help but she **5**........................ (tell) me to go and do my homework. I **6**........................ (explain) that luckily the teacher **7**........................ (not give) us any homework! Together we **8**........................ (make) a delicious dinner using the barbecue and the microwave – we **9**........................ (almost / finish) when her friends **10**........................ (arrived). Everything was OK!

3 Choose the correct adjectives to complete the blog post.

This year's school trip

At the end of each school year we have a class trip. It's usually quite **1bored / boring** – we go to a museum or to the cinema in town. But this year was different. We were **2surprised / surprising** to hear that the school had organised a hiking trip. We were going to see an **3amazed / amazing** waterfall which is famous in our region.

When we got off the minibus to start the hike, we were all **4excited / exciting** because no one had walked to the waterfall before. It took two hours to get to the viewpoint, but when we got there, we weren't **5disappointed / disappointing**. The waterfall was really beautiful and also very noisy! It was a bit **6frightened / frightening** to stand at the top and look down at all that water.

We had a rest and ate our lunch. Then it was time to walk back down to the car park. For a moment we were **7worrying / worried** that it might rain, but we were lucky and it didn't. When we got back to the bus, we all agreed that we were very **8tired / tiring**, but happy. The trip was a lot of fun.

4 Match the sentence halves (1–6) with (A–F) to complete each sentence.

1 She's so confident, ...
2 Jake sounded so relaxed on the phone, ...
3 My mum is disappointed ....
4 Isaac was nervous during his first driving lesson ....
5 I'm so excited, I can't speak! ....
6 Patrick felt guilty for shouting at his sister, ...

A I'm very jealous of his holiday.
B but he stayed calm and did well.
C I'm surprised she didn't want to sing on stage.
D but she could be so annoying!
E This concert is going to be amazing!
F because I found the family sailing holiday boring.

5 Grace wants to find out about her grandmother's childhood. Write her questions. Use the correct form of *used to*.

1 where / live?
....
2 walk / to school?
....
3 what sports / play?
....
4 where / go / after school?
....
5 have / a lot of homework?
....
6 what / enjoy / studying at school?
....

6 Grace's grandmother is answering her questions. Complete what she says with the correct form of *used to* and the verbs in brackets.

We **1**........................ (live) in a very small cottage near the sea. There were four of us children, so we **2**........................ (share) a room. But we **3**........................ (not mind). We had a lot of fun. We **4**........................ (catch) the bus to school because there wasn't a school in the village in those days. After school we **5**........................ (go) down to the beach and do some fishing or go swimming in the summer. Sometimes we played football, too. We **6**........................ (not watch) TV or play computer games like you do.

We **7**........................ (not have) as much homework as you children do nowadays, though. I remember I **8**........................ (like) science best at school. Maybe that's why I became a chemistry teacher!

REVIEW: UNITS 1-9

1 Find one extra word in each sentence.

1 I enjoyed the play which we saw it at the theatre.
2 What would you do if you have had more free time?
3 Everyone in my family loves to singing.
4 My parents have a newspaper is delivered every morning.
5 Tom told to his parents that he wanted to stay at a friend's house.
6 The temperature will be increase this afternoon.
7 You must to go to the dentist about your toothache.
8 We have a family trip to the beach from now and then.

2 Complete the crossword. The first letter of each word is given.

```
                              1
                              e
            2       3
            c       t □ □ □
  4     5
  g     s
                        6
                        d
  7
  s □ □ □ □ □ □

                  8
                  w □ □ □
```

Across

3 We went to London on the train today. It was a fun t............................ .
7 You need at least a week for s............................ in New York because there are so many interesting places to visit.
8 We watched the surfers riding the w............................ in the sea.

Down

1 Can you e............................ this maths problem to me? I don't understand it.
2 The tennis players walked onto the c............................ and started to play.
4 My phone alarm g............................ off at six every morning.
5 The actress walked onto the s............................ and everyone went quiet.
6 If there's a d............................ with our train, we'll have time to go to the café for lunch.

3 Choose the correct words to complete the letter.

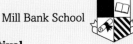

Mill Bank School

School trip to the Edinburgh Festival

Dear Parents and Students,

All students ¹**required / are required** to be at the school at 8.30 a.m. as the coach ²**leave / will leave** at 9 a.m. Students who arrive late **are having to / will have to** miss the trip and take classes instead.

When we first booked this trip, the coach company said that students ³**can / could** eat their packed lunch on the coach. However, they ⁴**have / had** recently decided that this is no longer possible. The coach driver ⁵**is going to make / makes** a stop along the journey so that students can eat their packed lunches in a pretty forest area.

Everything at the festival is free, so students ⁶**don't need to / didn't have to** take large amounts of cash with them. As it'll be a warm day, they ⁷**would / should** take a few pounds for drinks but nothing more.

Students ⁸**must / can** return to the car park by 4.45 p.m. The coach will leave at 5 p.m. and arrive back at the school at 9 p.m.

We hope everybody has a great day.

Mr Hiller

Head Teacher

4 Choose the correct definition for the words in bold.

1 I can only make a meal if I follow a **recipe**.
   A instructions for a meal
   B a pan for cooking food

2 Let's walk along the **cliff** top.
   A large area of rock with a steep side
   B area of sand or stones at the edge of the sea

3 I really want a new phone. This one's **ancient**!
   A old-fashioned
   B very old

4 I'm **anxious** about my science test. I don't think I did well.
   A worried
   B depressed

5 This meat is **disgusting**. I don't think I can eat it.
   A very different
   B extremely unpleasant

6 Our team got the **prize** for best presentation.

    A high marks in a test

    B something that says you did well in a competition

7 The final **destination** of our tour was the art museum.

    A a place you're going to

    B a place you're leaving

8 The city's never very **lively** on a Sunday evening.

    A full of people

    B exciting with lots of things happening

5 Choose the correct words to complete the sentences.

1 Jack and Dan don't like **keeping fit / online gaming**. They prefer doing sport outside.

2 We haven't got any homework tonight! Let's **chill out / join in** at the beach.

3 Everyone in the **orchestra / choir** sang really well.

4 We walked along the long, narrow cliff **path / field** and looked out onto the ocean.

5 There was an early morning **cloud / fog**, which meant we couldn't see much.

6 There's a festival in the park. Why don't you go and **join in / hang out with** the fun?

7 Where's the remote **machine / control**? I want to change the channel.

8 Grace is saving for a new camera. She's **mad / keen** about taking photos.

6 Complete the conversation with the correct form of the verbs in brackets.

A: You look fed up.

B: I am. I ^{1}............................ (go) into town this morning with Gemma because we ^{2}............................ (arrange) to do a babysitting course. Gemma ^{3}............................ (already / do) some babysitting but I haven't and I wanted to know more about it.

A: So what happened?

B: By the time we got there, the course ^{4}............................ (start). The teacher said that the course was full and we couldn't join.

A: What ^{5}............................ (you / do)?

B: We ^{6}............................ (ask) them to check their computer. There was a mistake on their system.

A: Oh no!

B: Yes, well, I'm not surprised. When I booked it, the receptionist ^{7}............................ (check) her phone the whole time! She ^{8}............................ (not pay) attention to me. Apparently, she ^{9}............................ (not book) us onto a babysitting course. She ^{10}............................ (book) us onto a course in flower arranging but we didn't want to do that! The next babysitting course ^{11}............................ (start) on the twenty-fourth, so we ^{12}............................ (probably / do) it then.

7 Complete the sentences with these words. You do not need two of the words.

beautiful   bossy   calm   depressing   fed up
guilty   narrow   relaxing

1 I always have a long bath after a stressful day. It's so ....

2 I don't think we can drive down this street. It's too ....

3 You never get angry. You're always so ....

4 We swam in the pool below the .... , high waterfall.

5 You're so .... ! Stop telling me what to do!

6 Have you done something you shouldn't? You look ....

7 Why do you listen to this sad music? It's so ....

8 I'm .... with doing the same thing every day. I want to do something different!

8 **e** Read the article and write one word for each gap.

The boy who **built his own** fairground ride

When Brendan Humphries was twelve years old, he decided to build a roller coaster ride in his own back garden in Sydney, Australia. He got ^{1}............................ idea after seeing online videos of similar, smaller projects. He liked those, but he wanted to create a bigger ^{2}............................ . Four years later and it ^{3}............................ now finally finished. Brendan wanted to make something similar to the roller coasters you find at theme parks, so his ride has a theme: it looks and feels like a railroad ^{4}............................ once existed in old Australian towns.

Surprisingly, Brendan ^{5}............................ never taken an engineering class in his life. He built the ride by trying things out and seeing what worked. He had ^{6}............................ test the different sections himself, so he has had a few crashes over the years, but nothing serious. Friends and family can now ride the entire roller coaster. Well done, Brendan!

10 Practice test

READING

Part 1

Questions 1–5

For each question, choose the correct answer.

 1

Unless you have provided a deposit, please return all books before the summer vacation.

A All students must give back their books before the start of the holidays.

B Students who have paid money can keep books over the holidays.

C Students will receive money back when they return their books.

 2

No one is permitted to use this lift while the fire alarm is ringing.

A People are not allowed to use the lift when the fire alarm sounds.

B People should exit the lift if the fire alarm goes off.

C People are unable to use the lift at any time.

84

(3)

 ✕

Don't forget to ask your parents to sign and date your end-of-year reports. Please return them before the end of the week.

A It is necessary for parents to bring signed reports to school.

B It is essential that signed reports are returned any day up to Friday.

C It is important that students sign and return their reports on Friday.

(4)

The student changing rooms are currently unavailable. The staff changing rooms are therefore open to all students.

A Students are allowed to use the staff changing rooms.

B Students can choose which changing rooms to use.

C Staff are unable to use the student changing rooms.

(5)

The school chess club is looking for new players to join the team next year. Previous experience not required. Training will be provided to the whole team.

A New players are wanted even if they have not played before.

B A teacher is needed to give training to the team.

C Only new members to the team will receive special training.

Part 2

Questions 6–10

For each question, choose the correct answer.

The five young people below want a part-time job over the summer holidays. On the next page are descriptions of eight available summer jobs. Decide which job would be the most suitable for the people below.

6 Marcia's really sociable and likes spending time with other people. She also enjoys baking. In the holidays she looks after her little brother from Monday to Friday, so is only available to work at weekends.

7 Danny is going to run a marathon, so he spends his days training. However, he's free in the evenings. He enjoys being outside and doesn't want to be kept inside at work.

8 Ellie wants to work for a few hours a week. She doesn't want to work at weekends. She enjoys spending time in nature and she's happy to work on her own.

9 Billy would like a job where he can be active outside. He wants to earn as much money as possible so that he can buy a new bike. He's happy to work hard.

10 Yasmin is crazy about anything related to food. She hopes to work during the week as she wants to spend Sundays with her family. She's shy and doesn't want to work with customers.

Job Advertisements

A Kitchen assistant required

We need a part-time assistant to work in the small kitchen of our hotel restaurant. The job involves preparing food before the restaurant opens and then cleaning the dishes after we have served the food. We require someone to work three hours Tuesday to Saturday, and Friday and Saturday evenings. We offer good pay.

B Dog sitter needed

We'd like to employ a local dog sitter to look after our two dogs for one hour a day Monday to Friday. We'd like you to take the dogs for a walk through the woods and then feed them when they return home. We're looking for a responsible, independent person.

C Waiter/Waitress wanted

We're looking for a friendly, hard-working person to serve customers at our Italian café. You will greet customers, take orders, serve food and clear away dishes and plates. We'd like you to work all day Thursday to Sunday each week, with other hours possibly available. Our staff are fun and great to work with.

D Gardener required

Gardener needed for weekend work to help keep our garden clean and tidy. You will need to cut the grass, water plants and do some general tidying. We're looking for someone who enjoys physical work and is happy to work alone. This job would suit a student interested in the environment.

E Farm assistant required

The position of farm assistant is available over the summer period. The job involves picking fruit for several hours per day and assisting with the packing of the fruit before it is sent for delivery. You must be fit and happy to work outdoors for long periods of time. No previous experience needed. We offer a good salary.

F Care home assistant wanted

A young person is wanted to work at our care home for four hours on Saturday and Sunday afternoons. The job requires you to make tea and fetch snacks for our elderly residents, as well as sit and chat to them. All our assistants must have basic kitchen skills.

G Furniture delivery person wanted

Do you want to keep fit? Do you enjoy varied work? Are you willing to work many hours a week? If so, then apply for the job of delivery person at our furniture shop. We deliver large pieces of furniture to customers, so you'll need to be physically strong and happy to travel out of the area.

H Weekly delivery person needed

We're looking for a fit, healthy person to deliver our weekly newspaper to over 100 homes in the Dilton area. You must be able to walk or cycle over three miles while pulling a shopping trolley full of newspapers in all kinds of weather. The job takes around three hours per week. We're happy for you to do it after 6 p.m.

Part 3

Questions 11–15

For each question, choose the correct answer.

....

> # Selling jewellery
>
> **Lily Richards shares her experience of starting her own business when she was still a teenager.**
>
> I was sixteen years old when I first thought about making jewellery. My mum recommended that I get a part-time job over the summer holidays and so I did some babysitting. However, it didn't pay very well and I soon began looking for something else. I think what motivated me was money. I was determined to buy a car so that I could learn to drive. I thought I could make and sell jewellery after my mum received a gorgeous handmade bracelet from a friend for her birthday.
>
> The first thing I did was make a shopping list of things I needed to buy. Shopping for them with my mum was definitely the most fun part. I then tried to make a necklace. Watching videos of jewellery makers online helped a bit but my first tries were rubbish, so I decided to take a course at a local college. With the teacher's help, I made fewer errors then started to get better. It took some time but I finally made something that I was proud of. I gave it to my friend Jade for her birthday. She loved it and that gave me the confidence to carry on.
>
> I spent hours making different types of jewellery – all my own designs. I showed them to some of my friends and family online, and they offered to buy them from me. That's when my business started. I made more pieces and gave them to my friends and family to sell. They held parties and sold them to their guests at a fairly cheap price. My mum and I also sold some at a really popular market during the summer holidays. That's when my jewellery started to get noticed.
>
> I soon realised I needed to pick a company name. I chose Purple Leaf Jewellery. I'd like to say that the name is made up of my favourite colour plus my favourite natural object. However, the truth is that I used a website that recommends names you can use. Friends made lots of suggestions and voted for their favourite but in the end I didn't go with any of those. I didn't listen to my brother either. He wanted me to name it after him!

11 Lily says she became interested in making jewellery because
- **A** she planned to give someone a gift.
- **B** she wanted to save money.
- **C** her mum suggested it to her.
- **D** her ambition was to become a designer.

12 At first, Lily thought the best thing about making jewellery was
- **A** getting tips from experts.
- **B** learning from her mistakes.
- **C** going to the store to buy materials.
- **D** showing her creations to family.

13 Lily thinks her jewellery started to become popular because
- **A** she advertised it on social media.
- **B** buyers were allowed to decide how the jewellery looked.
- **C** she chose a reasonable price for customers.
- **D** she sold the jewellery in a particular place.

14 How did Lily choose the name of her company?
- **A** She found it online.
- **B** She used words she liked.
- **C** She asked her friends.
- **D** She talked to family members.

15 Which of these things is Lily likely to say about starting a company?
- **A** 'It was too difficult and I wouldn't do it again.'
- **B** 'It's something you can do quickly.'
- **C** 'I'm so happy that my childhood hobby became my job.'
- **D** 'It's possible to achieve your dream.'

Part 4

Five sentences have been removed from the article below. For each question, choose the correct answer. There are three extra sentences which you do not need to use.

My summer of adventure

Last summer I had the most amazing experience. I went on a sailing trip from the UK to France. It was organised by a charity and I was offered one of six places. There were twelve people on board in total. Half of us were teenagers. **16**........ We were all there to work.

I'd never been on a boat before that trip and I was feeling nervous. What if I got seasick and couldn't help? I'd be so embarrassed. **17**........ I was absolutely fine the whole time. We spent half of the first day on land learning about safety rules and how to sail the ship. Then we got on board and started our journey.

The weather wasn't great at first. It was wet and windy but as the day went on, the sun came out and the wind slowed. **18**........ That made our trip slower but easier.

My first job was to help steer the ship in the right direction. We were all expected to do the different jobs around the ship over the five days. **19**........ I didn't mind doing that but some of the other kids didn't feel the same. They only wanted to do the exciting stuff, not boring housework.

In the evenings we had time to relax. When we arrived in France, we spent the day at the beach. We had a barbecue and played some games. **20**........ It was a lot of fun.

All in all, I had a great time. I met some cool people and learnt some new skills. I'd definitely recommend it.

A Neither of us had done it before.

B Everyone enjoyed the beach bowling in particular.

C The others were experienced adult sailors.

D They didn't all come from the same place.

E That meant they had a variety of work.

F Luckily, I wasn't ill at all.

G That included cooking and cleaning.

H It stayed fairly calm for the rest of the trip.

Part 5

Questions 21–26

For each question, choose the correct answer.

....

Are long summer holidays good?

In some countries, the summer holidays are just a few weeks long. In others, they can **21**........ almost three months. So which is better?

The main **22**........ about long summer holidays is memory. When students go on holiday for several weeks, they forget what they have studied. When they come back to school for the new term, teachers have to spend time **23**........ old topics with them.

Of course, longer holidays mean more time to relax. Students and teachers work hard during the school year. Long summer holidays give them the **24**........ to get some energy back. When everyone returns to school, they feel ready to start again.

Longer school holidays also give young people time to do things outside of school. They can **25**........ new places, try new activities and have new experiences. All of these things are **26**........ to a child's development.

21	**A** go	**B** exist	**C** last	**D** run
22	**A** worry	**B** reason	**C** chance	**D** problem
23	**A** knowing	**B** reviewing	**C** searching	**D** understanding
24	**A** access	**B** choice	**C** hope	**D** opportunity
25	**A** check	**B** travel	**C** explore	**D** question
26	**A** key	**B** urgent	**C** large	**D** necessary

Part 6

Questions 27–32

For each question, write the correct answer. Write one word for each gap.

My summer project

I wanted to do something useful during my summer holidays, so I decided to set myself a project: to open a youth club in my town. There used to **27**........................... one but it closed. The building was still there but it was empty. I wanted to reopen it.

I contacted hundreds of local companies and asked **28**........................... to give some money to the project. A lot of the people I spoke to said 'no' **29**........................... first, so I visited them and gave a presentation. Eventually, some said 'yes'.

I worked with someone from our local council. We used the money to repair the building and buy furniture and equipment **30**........................... as a pool table and a coffee machine. I asked some adults I knew to help me look after the club. They were happy **31**........................... do this.

Four months **32**........................... the club opened and a lot of my friends came. It looked great and I felt proud.

WRITING

Part 1

You *must* answer this question. Write your answer in about 100 words.

Question 1

Read this email from your English teacher and the notes you have made.

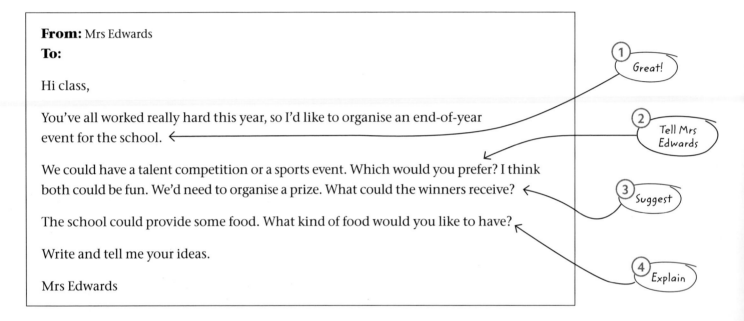

From: Mrs Edwards
To:

Hi class,

You've all worked really hard this year, so I'd like to organise an end-of-year event for the school. ←   ① Great!

We could have a talent competition or a sports event. Which would you prefer? I think both could be fun. We'd need to organise a prize. What could the winners receive? ←   ② Tell Mrs Edwards

The school could provide some food. What kind of food would you like to have? ←   ③ Suggest

Write and tell me your ideas.

Mrs Edwards

   ④ Explain

Write your email to Mrs Edwards, using all the notes.

Part 2

Choose ONE of these questions.

Write your answer in about 100 words.

....

Question 2

You see this announcement on an English-speaking website.

> **Articles wanted!**
>
> What helps you relax? Write an article telling us about
> the things you do to relax when you're feeling stressed.
> Do you think they're good things to do? Why?
>
> We'll read all your articles and publish the best one on
> our site.

Write your **article**.

Question 3

Your English teacher has asked you to write a story. Your story
must begin with this sentence.

When we heard the bell, we all ran.

Write your **story**.

LISTENING

Part 1

Questions 1–7

🔊 10.1 For each question, choose the correct answer.

---

1 Which job does the boy want to do?

A   B   C

2 Where did the girl get her new bag?

A   B   C

3 What is the prize for the winner of the radio competition?

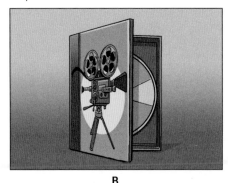

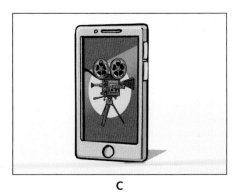

A   B   C

4 Which activity has the girl just done?

A

B

C

5 Which is the last lesson before the school holidays?

A

B

C

6 Where is the boy at the moment?

A

B

C

7 When does the girl have a job interview?

A

B

C

10 Practice test

Part 2

Questions 8–13

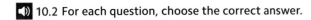 10.2 For each question, choose the correct answer.

8 You will hear two friends in a shop looking at mobile phones. What do they think about the silver phone?

   A The screen is too small.

   B It's too expensive.

   C It's not very attractive.

9 You will hear two friends talking about a problem at school. The boy advises his friend to

   A tell the truth.

   B forget about it.

   C say 'sorry'.

10 You will hear two friends who are lost. What do they decide to do?

   A call the girl's parents for help

   B look at a map

   C ask someone for directions

11 You will hear a girl talking to a friend about her holiday. What did she like best about it?

   A The food was very good.

   B The campsite was great.

   C The countryside was beautiful.

12 You will hear a brother and sister talking about studying for exams. The boy advises his sister to

   A start a study group with her friends.

   B study on her computer.

   C spend more time on difficult subjects.

13 You will hear two friends talking about babysitting. How do they both feel about it?

   A They want to get paid for it.

   B They think it's easy.

   C They are tired of it.

Part 3

Questions 14–19

🔊 10.3 For each question, write the correct answer in the gap. Write one or two words or a number or a date or a time.

You will hear a man called Sam telling a group of students about his work as a chef.

Being a chef

Sam's first job after school was **14**........................... in a restaurant kitchen.

Sam became a head chef after **15**........................... years.

Sam's responsibilities include buying **16**........................... as well as cooking and presenting food.

Sam needs a **17**........................... for his job.

Sam says one advantage of his career is being able to **18**........................... .

Sam would like to work on a **19**........................... in the near future.

Part 4

Questions 20–25

🔊 10.4 For each question, choose the correct answer.

You will hear an interview with a hospital nurse called Amy.

20 Amy wanted to work as a nurse because
  A she wanted to help people.
  B some of her family worked at the hospital.
  C she was interested in biology at school.

21 How did Amy feel on her first day as a nurse?
  A nervous because of her age
  B excited to start her job
  C worried that she would make a mistake

22 What makes Amy feel angry?
  A working long hours
  B people who waste her time
  C rude behaviour towards doctors and nurses

23 What does Amy like best about her job?
  A working in a team
  B every day being different
  C saving lives

24 In the future Amy plans to
  A get some more qualifications.
  B change to a different department.
  C continue to do her job well.

25 Amy advises anyone who wants to be a nurse to
  A get some work experience.
  B choose a good university course.
  C talk to people who have done the job.

SPEAKING

Part 1

Phase 1

🔊 10.5 The examiner is going to ask you some questions about you. Listen and answer the questions. Pause the recording after each beep and give your answer.

Phase 2

🔊 10.6 The examiner is going to ask some more questions about you. Listen and answer the questions. Pause the recording after each beep and give your answer.

Part 2

🔊 10.7 The examiner is going to give you a photo and ask you to talk on your own about it. Listen and follow the examiner's instructions. Speak for about a minute.

Part 3

🔊 10.8 The examiner is going to describe a situation to you and give you some pictures. You and the other student must talk about them together. Listen and follow the examiner's instructions. Talk together for about two minutes.

Jobs the girl could do

Part 4

🔊 10.9 Now the examiner is going to ask you some questions about the topic of the pictures in Part 3. Listen and answer the questions. Pause the recording after each beep and give your answer.

AUDIOSCRIPTS

S.1

A = Ann   B = Ben

A: Hi! Did you have a good weekend?

B: Yes, I did, thanks. I went horse-riding for the first time.

A: Wow! Where did you do that?

B: In the countryside near my uncle's village. It was amazing! I had to wear a special helmet and riding boots.

A: I'd love to try horse-riding. But it sounds a bit scary!

B: It's not. Well, at least I wasn't scared – I was on the horse with my uncle. Although, I nearly fell off the horse at one point! It wanted to run but, luckily, my uncle was in control, so it couldn't go too fast.

1.1 and 1.2

J = Jess   A = Amelia

J: Hi, Amelia. How are you?

A: Oh hi, Jess. I'm fine, thanks. It's so good to hear from you. It seems as if you're in the next room, not thousands of miles away in Australia! How are things?

J: Great, thanks.

A: Are you still at the hotel in Sydney?

J: No, I'm staying with my aunt and uncle now.

A: Where do they live? Is it very different from Manchester?

J: Are you joking? It's completely different here. They live on the Gold Coast and the weather is fantastic. It's still hot and sunny even though it's nearly six o'clock.

A: I don't believe it! It's raining here in Manchester. What are you doing at the moment?

J: Well, I'm having dinner in the garden. They've got a huge garden and they're building a swimming pool now.

A: What's that noise?

J: It's a kookaburra bird. We hear them all the time in the garden. Hang on a minute – I'm holding the phone out now.

A: Wow! They don't sound like British birds at all!

J: I know! I love it here. In the evenings we sometimes go to the beach, too. We have a swim and watch the sunset.

A: Well, at the moment I'm listening to the rain against the window and I feel jealous! But I'm really happy for you, too.

J: Thanks, Amelia.

A: Listen, I have to go because my dad's calling me. He's making breakfast this morning, and I think it's ready.

J: Oh yes, of course – I forgot about the time difference. Have a good day!

A: Have a good evening!

1.3

1   Fran is a very intelligent girl. I know that she worries a lot about the end-of-year test that's coming up, but she should be more positive about her chances.

2   I'm rather unhappy about Sam this term. He's always chatting with his friends in class. He needs to talk a bit less and do more work. He can make his plans for the weekend after class!

3   I'm afraid I had to get angry with Clare last week. She's often rude to me and I know that her other teachers are fed up with it too.

4   It's nearly exam time and Alex needs to take a lot more care with his work if he wants to get a good mark. He does it too quickly and he doesn't check it before he hands it in.

5   I was so impressed with Isobel recently. We went out for the day to the forest and she had a nasty fall. She didn't panic or start crying – she just patiently waited for help.

6   Nick is doing very well this term. He always does his homework. He's never late for school and I know that if I ask him to do something, he will always do it as well as he can.

1.4

N = Narrator

1

N: You will hear two friends talking about what to do next in a museum.

A: Where shall we go next?

B: I don't know about you, but I wouldn't mind looking at some paintings.

A: Really? I'm not sure.

B: Would you rather go to the Roman section to look at the coins? I saw them last time and they're really beautiful.

A: Yes, that sounds like a good idea. And I know you love collecting coins! What floor do we need to go to?

B: Um, upstairs to the second floor, I think – next to the gift shop.

2

N: You will hear two friends talking about travelling by bus.

A: The bus should be here in a few minutes.

B: Are we at the right stop? Are we going to be late?

A: Don't worry, we're at the right place. The bus is probably in some traffic. I'm at the bus station every day, remember? I take the bus to school I'm tired of taking it every single day, actually!

B: Are you? That's a shame. I love taking the bus – I guess it's because I don't often get the chance. Oh, I can't wait! I'd like to sit on the top deck; is that OK?

A: Yes, I'd like that too. I usually have to stand downstairs on the way to school in the morning.

B: Here it comes now!

3

N: You will hear two friends who are shopping for clothes.

A: Well, what do you think?

B: Hmm … Not sure I like it. I think I prefer the one you tried on before – the blue one.

A: Do you really?

B: Yes, it suited you better.

A: But you said you didn't like that one. You said it looked old-fashioned and too dark.

B: I know, I'm sorry. It looked better than this one, though. Do you know what?

A: What?

B: Why don't you take that off and try on a bigger one? I think this one's too tight.

A: Same colour?

B: Yeah, actually the colour's great. But you should ask if they have it in Large. It will look better with your jeans.

4

N: You will hear two friends trying to find their way in a shopping centre.

A: Where are we? I always get lost in these places!

B: I know what you mean. Once you're inside it's difficult to know where you are.

A: Are the cash machines on the second floor?

B: I don't think so. Let's look at this map.

A: We're here, I think … Oh, there's an information desk. Maybe we can try asking there.

B: We've just walked past it – it's closed on Sundays. We should try using the interactive map.

A: Where is it?

B: It's over there next to the lift, look. It's touch-screen and it shows you exactly where you are, in 3D!

A: Great idea! Come on, let's go.

5

N: You will hear two friends choosing a film to see.

A: Hi, how are things?

B: Good, thanks. Have you had any ideas about what we should watch?

A: I had a look at the cinema website online, but there's so much choice. I don't know … What do you feel like?

B: There's that new science fiction film – what's it called again? Something about 'The Stars'?

A: Yeah, I know the one. I don't like science fiction much and I hate the actor. He's terrible.

B: Oh, I love science fiction! Um, OK, what about something funny, then? A comedy?

A: Hmm … I'm not sure. Shall we watch that action film about pilots? I saw a video the other day about how they made it, and I really want to see it.

B: Yeah, I like those too. Let's go for that one, then.

6

N: You will hear two friends talking about a café they often go to.

A: Brill Coffee looks so different now, doesn't it?

B: Yes, I liked it the way it was.

A: Did you? Why?

B: It just seemed brighter. Why have they put all these paintings on the walls and changed the tables?

A: I think they wanted to make it a bit more homely, you know? That's why they've put the new sofas in the corner with the cushions. I think I prefer the new look, actually.

B: Well, I don't mind what it looks like, as long as they're still making those delicious sandwiches!

A: You're right! Let's hope they haven't changed the menu as well.

1.5

M = Man   S = Sophie

1

M: What's your surname?

S: Taylor.

2

M: What's your middle name?

S: Maria.

3

M: What's your address?

S: 74 Clarence Street, Weybridge.

4

M: How do you spell the name of the town?

S: W–E–Y–B–R–I–D–G–E.

5

M: What's your postcode?

S: KT13 7ZH.

6

M: Can you spell your email address, please?

S: S–O–P–H–I–E–T at H–I–T–H–E–R–E dot com.

1.6

1 What's your surname?
2 What's your middle name?
3 What's your address?
4 How do you spell the name of the town?
5 What's your postcode?
6 Can you spell your email address, please?

1.7

W = Woman   A = Anton

W: Where do you live?

A: I'm from Odessa. It's a big city in Ukraine, but it's not the capital.

W: And what's your favourite thing about living there?

A: Well, one reason I love Odessa is because it's a beautiful city. There are some amazing buildings – for example, the Opera and Ballet Theatre.

W: Do you live with your family?

A: Yes – with my parents and my two brothers. I get on well with my brothers and I enjoy spending time with them. Maybe it's because we like doing the same things.

W: What do you like doing in the summer?

A: We all enjoy water sports, so we go canoeing or swimming in the sea.

W: What about in the winter?

A: In the winter we also go to the sea, but we go for long walks along the beach.

2.1

1 Hmm, I think I was chatting to my friend Ali on my phone then.

2 I was at a friend's house and we were learning some new English words ready for a test at school today. We weren't doing a great job, though!

3 8 o'clock? I was with my sister. We were having dinner and, for once, we weren't arguing!

4 I was coming home from football. It was raining and I was standing at the bus stop getting wet.

5 I think my brother was telling me about something but I wasn't listening – as usual! Sorry, little bro!

6 My friend and I were watching a film. I can't remember the name but I know I wasn't enjoying it very much.

7 I was talking to my parents while they were making dinner. They were asking me about my day.

8 8 o'clock? Oh yeah, I was sleeping. I fell asleep while I was doing my homework!

2.2 and 2.3

1

A: How many languages do you speak?

B: Two – English and Arabic.

2

A: How do you pronounce this word?

B: You say it like this: bother.

A: Bother. Great, thanks!

3

A: I didn't hear what the teacher said. Can you explain what we need to do?

B: Sure. First, we have to do exercise 1 on page 23.

4

A: I don't know this word. What does it mean?

B: 'Very big.'

A: Oh right, thanks.

5

A: Turn right at the end of this road. Then turn left and then left again. You'll see the hospital on the right.

B: I'm sorry, I didn't catch all that. Could you repeat it, please?

6

A: Our new teacher has a really strange accent.

B: Yes, I agree. I don't always understand him.

2.4

1 I'm so sorry I'm late. The bus didn't come, so I got a taxi but I still got stuck in traffic.

2 I'm calling to tell you about the awful service I got in one of your shops today. The lady serving me was very rude – I didn't buy anything because she wouldn't help me!

3 Hi, Greg! It's me, Sam. We met at Anya's birthday party last year. How are you?

4 A: … so, we went to the beach and then we …
   B: Sorry but the lesson's going to start in a minute. We need to go.

5 So, I need to get milk, bread and a new notebook. Hmm … if I go to the supermarket, I should be able to get it all from there. OK, time to go.

6 In my view, the book was amazing but the film was disappointing.

7 So, English is a stress-timed language, which means that not every syllable in a sentence is stressed. Some are stressed and some aren't.

2.5 and 2.6

Knowing how to program a computer is a very useful skill these days. That's why we've developed an online course for you. A lot of similar courses teach you the skills you need to design a game, but on our ten-hour online course you will learn how to build apps.

The course provides you with some short films explaining how to do different things. You then try those things yourself with some practice activities. We could give you a test, but we think that would be unkind!

Many online courses are expensive. You can pay over £1,000 for the longer ones. With our course, the teachers all give their time for free, so there's just a small fee of £10 to cover the costs of running our website. That's just a week or two of pocket money!

At the end of the course, you'll receive an email to say that you've completed the ten hours. If you choose to do the course assignment, you'll also get a certificate to show that you passed the course. This will be a good thing to add to your CV when you finish your studies.

If you don't like the idea of an online course, there are some one-day face-to-face sessions that you can attend here in the city some weekends. Local companies arrange them at one of the colleges.

If you attend one of the face-to-face sessions, and you're not yet a teenager, you'll need to have a parent with you. Anyone who attends might want to take their own laptop. However, you don't have to because there are laptops and tablets available for you to use.

AUDIOSCRIPTS

2.7

1 One of the people is wearing a cap on their head.

2 In the foreground, there are some skateboards and two bikes.

3 Three of the teenagers are sitting on a wall.

4 In the background, there are some blocks of flats or buildings.

5 I think that the three people on the right are listening to the boy on the left.

6 I think that the photo wasn't taken inside. It was taken outside.

7 There are four people in the photo.

8 Two of the people have long hair. The other two have short dark hair.

9 The boy on the right is sitting on the ground.

10 The girl dressed in a white top has got a pair of headphones around her neck.

3.1

J = Jon   T = Tim   A = Assistant

J: Where are you going, Tim?

T: To the computer shop. I'm going to buy a new game.

J: I'm bored. I'll come with you.

T: OK. The game I want is quite new, so it won't take long to find it.

T: Ah, here it is. There's no price on it. *[to shop assistant:]* Excuse me, how much is this?

A: Let me check. This one's forty-five euros but we're going to have a sale soon, so it'll probably be cheaper then.

T: Thanks! I won't buy it today then.

J: I'm going to meet my friend in town next weekend. I can get it for you then if you like.

T: Oh that would be great – thanks, Jon.

3.2 and 3.3

G = Grace   C = Charlotte

G: Hi, Charlotte. How are things on holiday?

C: Great, thanks, except that at the weekend, the power went off for two days!

G: Oh no! What did you do?

C: Well, we went out during the day to the beach but the evenings were difficult.

G: I can imagine.

C: I mean, we couldn't heat any food because the microwave wasn't working, and we couldn't cook because the oven wouldn't work either. The local cafés couldn't open because they had the same problem as us.

G: Oh dear! What did you eat?

C: We ate cold stuff from the fridge-freezer. We didn't starve. Of course, we had to wash our plates by hand in cold water because we couldn't use the dishwasher. That wasn't so bad because we didn't have any dirty pans or anything. The main problem was that I couldn't plug in my phone, so the battery died. And the wi-fi shut off too, of course, so there was no internet!

G: Oh no, that's really bad. How did you cope?

C: Well, there wasn't much I could do. We spent the evenings playing cards by candlelight. It was kind of fun at first but after an hour or two it got boring. Honestly, I had no idea how much we need electricity! I was so happy when it came back on.

3.4

N = Narrator

1

N: What will the girl buy from the shop?

A: So, what do you need in here?

B: Well, I'd like to get some new headphones but I'm not sure this is the best place to buy them. I can get them cheaper online.

A: OK, so what else?

B: My mum's given me money for some new speakers, so I should get some of those. I think they're over there. I'd also quite like a keyboard for my tablet – typing with that would make my homework easier. Unfortunately, I don't have enough money for one at the moment.

2

N: What will the boy use to do his homework?

A: What's our English homework?

B: We have to write a news article on a topic of our choice.

A: Oh yeah. Have you done yours?

B: Yes, I handed it in yesterday. I used a local newspaper to come up with some topics.

A: I already have an idea, so I don't need that. Do we need to take photos to include in the article?

B: I don't think so, but you might want to use an online dictionary to check your spelling. You'll lose marks if it's wrong.

A: Good idea. I'll do that.

3

N: Which type of game is the girl's favourite?

A: So, what kind of games do you like?

B: I'm not keen on those animal games – the ones with magic and stuff. They are better for younger kids – I think they're really boring!

A: I know what you mean.

B: I sometimes play sports games. I can beat my older brother at racing games, which really annoys him! I like simple games best, though – like ones where you shoot at little circles so they disappear, for example. I spend hours playing those kinds of games on my phone.

4

N: Who does the boy want to see in concert?

A: I'm trying to get tickets to see my favourite band.

B: Is that the girl band from the TV talent show?

A: Yes!

B: They annoy me. They pretend to be really good friends but they've only just met. You should see that new rock band. I saw them last month. Their songs are great.

A: I've heard that a famous DJ is playing here in the summer. The one who's number one at the moment.

B: Really? Oh wow, we have to go! I'd love to see him live!

5

N: What website does the girl use most often?

A: Have you seen this football website? It's great.

B: Oh yeah, I go on there all the time. I probably go on there more than any other site.

A: I like this music site too. Have you seen it?

B: Yes. I find the articles a bit boring. I prefer listening to music to reading about it. It's the same with all these blogs people write. I prefer having my own experiences to reading about other people's. I don't go on those kinds of sites much at all.

6

N: What machine has broken down?

A: What's wrong?

B: I'm annoyed. I put all the plates and dishes in the dishwasher this morning but I forgot to switch it on. My mum won't be happy!

A: Oh dear!

B: That's not the worst thing. The washing machine isn't working, so I have no clean sports clothes for our sports lesson later.

A: You can come to my house at lunchtime and borrow some of my brother's stuff. He won't mind. And we can cook some chips in the microwave and have them for lunch!

B: OK, great. Thanks!

7

N: What time will the mobile phone shop open?

A: Do you know what time the mobile phone shop opens this morning? I dropped my phone yesterday and the screen broke. I want to get it fixed.

B: Well, they usually open at nine fifteen but it's Saturday today. I think they open half an hour earlier, at eight forty-five.

A: Oh right. Well, I guess if I walk to the bus stop at eight fifteen, I should get there at about the time they open. Then I can get my phone fixed and still enjoy the rest of the day.

3.5

A: Why don't we watch a film later?

B: Good idea. We should watch the latest Marvel film. I think Ben has the DVD.

A: We could download it – it's probably easier.

B: OK, good idea. Shall I do that now?

A: Yes. Then we can watch it when we want to. And we ought to get some popcorn. I'll go to the shop.

B: Great! How about getting some of that sweet and salty popcorn? I love that!

A: Sounds good. I'll see what they've got.

3.6 and 3.7

A: I think a tablet's useful. If you download a film onto it, you can watch it anywhere. It's really convenient.

B: That's true. And the screen's bigger than a mobile, so it's easier to see what's happening – but smartphones are easier to carry around. You might not want to take your tablet on a bus or something.

A: Yes, that's a good point. Maybe a tablet's useful for watching a film at home, then, rather than when you're out.

B: Yes. How about the home cinema? What do you think to that?

A: I think it's fantastic if you have the space. It's like having a private cinema!

B: You're right. I'd like a room like that. It's better to watch a film with other people, too.

A: Hmm, I'm not sure. I prefer to watch films alone. It's easier to concentrate when there aren't other people talking all the time – like my little sister!

B: So you don't think watching films on a laptop with friends is a good idea either?

A: Well, for me, laptops are great for video clips but they aren't so good for films.

B: I don't agree. In my view, it's more fun to watch films with other people because you can stop the film and talk about it.

A: Maybe. I don't mind the cinema because everyone has to be quiet and it's nice to go out and see something. It makes it more special. It's expensive, though, isn't it?

B: Yes, my mum's always telling me that!

3.8

1 I like watching films on my tablet with headphones. Do you?

2 I think documentaries are amazing, don't you?

3 It's best not to watch scary films before bed. Do you agree?

4 These days, cartoons aren't just for kids, are they?

4.1 and 4.2

A: Right. Have you ever helped with sports day before?

B: No, I haven't. Can you tell me what I have to do?

A: Um, yes. These are the things to do. I've already ticked some things off the list, but you can help with the rest. Let me see … I've washed the team vests. I did that last week.

B: Great. What about the medals?

A: No, I haven't bought the medals yet. Can you do that?

B: Yes, I can order them on the internet.

A: Good. I haven't written the team lists yet – but I'm going to do that tomorrow. Ah! Can you find the sacks for the jumping race? It's the one the parents take part in.

B: Where do I look?

A: Mrs Brown has already looked in the sports storeroom and they weren't there. You need to ask around and see if the sacks are in one of the other storerooms.

B: OK. Have you sent an email to the parents about sports day yet?

A: Yes. I sent an update on Monday with the times and a list of events.

B: That's great. What's the next thing on the list?

A: Er … check the sound system. Well, I've just done that. The sound system is fine.

B: OK.

A: But Mr Granger hasn't cut the grass yet. Can you ask him to cut it tomorrow, if it doesn't rain?

B: Will do.

A: Have I forgotten anything?

B: Mmm … I don't know. I'll let you know if I think of anything.

4.3

R = Reporter   T = Tom

R: So, Tom, how does it feel when people call you 'Tom Lewis – super-fan'?

T: I don't mind. I quite like being a 'super-fan'. I am very keen on my football, it's true. I always have been, since I can remember.

R: Have you got a favourite place to watch football?

T: I think it's the new city stadium. It's amazing. When the crowd start singing Wesley Richards' name, you know, it's a great place to be.

R: Is that your favourite player at the moment?

T: Yes, the captain of the team, Wesley Richards. He's playing very well right now.

R: What makes him such a good player?

T: He's a great athlete. He trains very hard.

R: And could you choose your favourite football moment? What has been the best moment you've experienced so far?

T: That's a tough question … I think watching the cup final at Wembley two years ago. I had a great seat in the front row that day.

R: Lucky you! And I hear that you have collected quite a lot of football material over the years. What's the best souvenir in your collection?

T: I think it's my medal from the World Cup in Argentina. It's more than forty years old and it was difficult to find.

R: Well, Tom, thanks very much for talking to me today. Enjoy today's match!

T: Thanks a lot.

4.4 and 4.5

I = Interviewer   R = Ryan

I: Today I'm speaking to young gymnast Ryan Johnson. Ryan, it's great to meet you.

R: Hi!

I: So, do you enjoy going to the gym six days a week?

R: Well, there are days when I really don't want to come to the gym, and I have to push myself to get out of bed. But most of the time, I don't want to be anywhere else. It's hard work, but it makes me feel good about myself.

I: What would you say is the most difficult thing about gymnastics training?

R: Well, the early mornings are hard sometimes – especially after a hard day at school. But I'd say watching what you eat is more difficult – you really need to look after your body if you want to be the best. Other gymnasts find the pressure of training for competitions the hardest – but not me. I'm good at dealing with that!

I: Why did you start doing gymnastics, Ryan?

R: At home, we used to watch gymnastics on TV all the time but what really got me into it was watching my older sister take part in competitions – she's a gymnast too. I'd watch her and think, 'I could do that!' I had to go to the gym with her, anyway – my mum couldn't leave me at home. So I joined the training programme when I was five.

I: And what would you say motivates you the most?

R: Definitely _not_ medals – I don't really care about winning. What makes me want to keep going is watching older gymnasts do well. They are my heroes – I learn so much from them and want to be like them. My coach often says being a successful gymnast may also mean I'll be famous – and rich! – but I don't really care about that either.

I: And what is the most important factor in being a great gymnast?

R: It's the hours you spend training – the 'ten-thousand-hour rule'. My coach says that to become an expert in any sport, you need to train for ten thousand hours. That's over years and years, of course. Skill is very important too – I mean, if you have a natural talent for a sport, you're likely to be _really_ good at it! But the harder you train, the better you'll be!

I: What has gymnastics taught you?

R: Well, when you are competing, you spend a lot of time with different people, and you have to feel OK about being away from your family. So I think I'm much less shy than I used to be. The one thing I still need to get better at, though, is time management – with all the time I have to spend at the gym, I need to learn to manage my time better.

I: Well, Ryan, thanks so much for talking to me and good luck for the future!

4.6 and 4.7

Well, it's a photo of two teenagers. They're in the countryside and they're climbing. They're wearing special clothes and one of them is wearing a special hat – I think it's called a helmet? At the back there are some fields and trees. The boy who is sitting down is pulling something – um, I can't remember what it's called. Perhaps there's another person climbing with them – it might be a friend or a parent. The boys look very confident. They don't look frightened. And the activity looks really exciting – I'd love to try it.

4.8

1 The photo shows a girl and an older man doing an activity together.

2 They're playing with large plastic rings – I can't remember what they're called.

3 I can see lots of trees, so maybe they're in a park.

4 They're both wearing jeans and jumpers, so I don't think the weather is very hot.

5 It might be spring or autumn.

6 Perhaps the man at the back of the photo is the girl's grandfather.

7 They both look very happy – I think they're having a great time.

5.1

A: Eve, thanks for talking to Teen Time today. It's great to meet you.

B: Thanks!

A: You started acting when you were very young – just seven years old. Do you think that it was too young?

B: A lot of people ask me that. I wouldn't be an actor today if I didn't enjoy it. My parents didn't push me. I really wanted to act from a young age.

A: So, your parents don't mind?

B: No, they're really supportive. They look after me. And I think they would tell me if I needed to take a break.

A: So, you think it's OK to be famous when you are little?

B: Well, it's not right for everyone. If I had children, I wouldn't push them to be actors. It would be their decision. But I love acting. If I wasn't an actor, I would miss the excitement a lot.

A: Do you have any hopes or dreams for the future?

B: There are lots of actors I'd love to work with. If I could work with any actor, it would be Eddie Redmayne. I think he's great.

A: What would be your least favourite role?

B: I'm not that good at dancing. So I wouldn't want to be in a musical if I had to dance. But really, I am very lucky. I can't imagine doing anything else.

A: You don't want to be in pop music, like your brother?

B: No! Definitely not! But my brother says he would be in films if he wasn't a musician.

A: And what do you …

5.2

1

A: Good morning. It's a real pleasure to meet you. Are you ready to start?

B: Yes.

A: I sent you a list of questions last week. Are you happy to talk about those?

B: Yes, that's fine.

A: OK. Let's switch on the microphone.

2

A: Well, I'd better go home and start writing.

B: What did you think?

A: It was OK, but not as good as I was expecting. I'm probably going to give it three stars.

3

A: I need to go through my part before our performance on Saturday.

B: I know, me too. I'm not sure of all the notes yet.

A: I think there's a room free at the studio. Shall I call them?

B: Yeah. Good idea.

4

A: OK. Shall we go in? Have you got your lyrics?

B: It's fine. I know them already.

A: Great. You go into the studio and put on your headphones. Then we'll check the microphone.

5

A: Move a bit to the left. OK. That's fine. We've got a view of Tower Bridge in the background now. Ready?

B: Yes.

A: OK. We're going live in five, four, three, two, one …

6

A: How do the shoes feel?

B: They're fine. Yeah. The costume is great. I'm just going to do my warm-up.

A: Great. Good luck out there!

5.3 and 5.4

N = Narrator

1

N: You will hear a girl talking about listening to music in her car.

A: How did you find out about that pop group? I've never heard of them.

B: I heard their new song on the radio in the car.

A: Do you always have music on in the car?

B: Yes, *always*! If I don't listen to music, I feel sick.

A: Really?!

B: Yes, I have to listen and concentrate on the road at the same time.

A: What do you do if you're in someone else's car?

B: I have to ask them to switch on some music as soon as we get in!

2

N: You will hear two friends talking about a concert.

A: That was good, don't you think?

B: It was, but I couldn't see the band very well. I was watching the screen a lot.

A: Me too. I was really disappointed – I didn't go to the concert to have to watch them on a screen! Next time let's go nearer the front.

B: Yeah. We'll know better next time!

A: I thought the concert went really quickly, though.

B: It did. I wanted them to play a couple more of their songs – you know, like *Travel in Time*.

A: I agree. That's my favourite.

3

N: You will hear two friends talking about listening to music on a smartphone.

A: Is that your new phone?

B: Yeah. What do you think? It's got lots of space for music.

A: It looks great. Have you got headphones for it? My parents don't let me listen to mine without headphones. They say it's rude. I guess it is.

B: Yeah, I think so too, to be honest. I've got some headphones, and a spare battery, too. The problem is that the music never sounds as good through headphones, does it?

A: Well, it depends. My headphones sound fine.

B: Can I try them?

A: Sure. I'll bring them when I come over at the weekend.

4

N: You will hear two friends talking about an album they listened to.

A: Thanks for telling me about that band. I think I'm going to download some songs from their new album.

B: Are you? Their new album is great. Which ones did you like best?

A: I really liked the second one. What's it called – *Butterfly Wings*? *Butterfly*? I can't remember the words, but the song is great.

B: Oh, I know which one you mean. It reminds me of something else, though.

A: Does it? I think it's really different and fresh.

B: It makes me think of another band – you know, it's a bit One Direction.

A: Really? I didn't think that. But I'll download it when I get home and have another listen.

5

N: You will hear two friends talking about listening to music while studying.

A: Do you always listen to music when you do your homework?

B: Yeah – not too loud, though. It helps me concentrate.

A: Yeah, me too – but not when I'm doing science. Or maths – I tend to focus on the music and forget about the numbers!

B: Really? It helps me remember things more easily, actually. Especially classical music. It's something about the style, the timing – I don't know. But it works – it somehow helps my brain 'record' important information!

A: Hmm … interesting. I've never listened to classical music before. I'll try it.

6

N: You will hear a girl talking about a music competition she has entered.

A: Ready for the big day?

B: I'm not sure, to be honest.

A: You're not worried about playing in front of an audience, are you?

B: Well, I'm not very keen on playing in front of people, but it's not that. It just seems a waste of time.

A: But you've worked so hard for this show. Hours and hours of practice!

B: I know, but I don't think I've got any better, really. And so many people have entered – they *must* be better than me. I'm just not good enough.

5.5

A: Have you signed up for guitar lessons?

B: Yes, I have. Have you?

A: Yeah. Are you going to buy a guitar or rent one?

B: I've rented one already. Then if I don't like the classes, I can just return it.

A: That's a good idea. I'll rent one too, in case I give up after a while. Where did you get yours from?

B: The music shop in town. I'd go there and try some different sizes if I were you. Then you'll get the best one for you.

A: Oh! I'll enjoy that. I always thought that you can't go in unless you're a real musician. Are all the guitars the same price?

B: Yes, they are, unless you choose a very fancy one.

A: Will you come with me tomorrow and help me choose, if you aren't busy?

B: OK! It'll be fun.

5.6

1 Look at object one. What does it look like?
2 Look at object two. What do you use it for?
3 Look at object three. What's it made of?
4 Look at object one. What do you use it for?
5 Look at object two. What's it made of?
6 Look at object three. What colour is it?

5.7

1 It looks like two spoons.
2 You use it for cleaning flutes.
3 It's made of leather.
4 You use it for playing music.
5 It's made of metal and plastic.
6 It's black.

5.8

A: What's happening in this photo? Is one of those boys your brother?

B: No, that's Aidan, my cousin. He's the one with long hair. I think he's playing in some kind of street music festival in this picture.

A: What's he playing? It looks like a drum, but he's holding it differently.

B: Yes, it is a type of drum. I can't remember what it's called, but it's an Irish instrument.

A: What's it made of?

B: Wood and animal skin, I think. You use that little stick to hit it, but you can use your fingers, too. Aidan can play it really quickly.

A: It looks like fun.

B: Yeah. I need to ask him to let me try next time I visit.

6.1

The Mountain View Resort was hit by a small avalanche yesterday. Guests were asked to stay in their rooms for several hours while the emergency services tried to reach them. They were given food and drinks by hotel staff, and children were provided with games. As this is an area which is often hit by avalanches, locals were able to keep guests calm. Everyone in the area was moved out of the resort during the evening and no missing people or serious injuries were reported. The area is still covered in large amounts of snow, and hotels will remain closed for at least a week.

6.2

clear sky
green grass
heavy snowfall
humid weather
narrow path
sandy beach
strong waves
thick fog

6.3 and 6.4

P = Presenter   L = Lucas

P: Today, I'm talking to Lucas who recently organised a rubbish run in his village. Lucas, what is a rubbish run and why did you organise it?

L: It's a race where people run and pick up rubbish from the streets at the same time. My mum and dad started to complain about the rubbish in the village last year, mostly from cars driving through. That's when I noticed it. I wanted to be happy that I lived in a pretty place, not sad I lived somewhere ugly. After the race, we won a 'Prettiest Village' award – but that wasn't why I did it.

P: The event was quite big. How did you feel on the day?

L: Well, before the event, I was worried about the really small things we needed to do. I didn't have time to look forward to it. On the day, though, I was really calm. I was sure the event would be successful. I loved watching everyone run.

P: And what did the 200 runners that took part like most about it?

L: Well, they said it was enjoyable and, of course, a useful way to clean the village. Above all, though, they liked the way it was planned – the fact that both adults and children could run the race and enjoy a good day out.

P: I hear that you're going to repeat the event next year. What will you do differently?

L: Well, I'll definitely set it up for a different weekend, probably one in early summer, to avoid the cold and the rain we had this year. Another idea is that we have a team race. I think that'll be too difficult to organise, though. I might also ask people to bring their own rubbish bags but I'm not sure yet.

P: What are your plans for the future?

L: I'd like to have a national clean-up day where events like this happen in villages, towns and cities everywhere. That'd be great. I used social media to tell people about my event. It'll be easy to use it to create interest in all the events.

P: And finally, what suggestions would you give other teenagers about our environment?

L: Well, young people like me know to throw their rubbish in a bin, so I won't say that. I think the important thing is that we all try to make a small change because if we all do that, it becomes a big change. You don't have to think of anything particularly new and amazing. Simple things can help.

6.5

Some students want to reduce plastic waste at their school. Here are some things they could encourage the school and the students to do. Talk together about the different things and say which would help to reduce plastic waste most.

6.6 and 6.7

D = Dylan   M = Marta

D: I think the school should provide more recycling bins. Do you agree?

M: Yes, I do. Um … Er …

D: Go on.

M: Yes, well, we definitely need to recycle more, and having more recycling bins will help.

D: Exactly. What do you think about the mugs?

M: They're better than throw away cups with plastic lids. The cafeteria shouldn't use those, really. Plastic lids are a waste and can't be recycled easily.

D: I agree, and we use so many of them. I also think the school needs to provide more water fountains, too. Then people won't need to buy bottles of water.

M: Yes, that's a good idea. And so is charging for plastic bags in the cafeteria, in my opinion.

D: Hmm … How would that help?

M: Well, if people had to pay, they'd stop using them.

D: Why do you think that?

M: Because we only use them when they're free.

D: Hmm, good point!

6.8

1 When you buy a drink, do you prefer a glass bottle or a plastic one?
2 Would you like to use less plastic?
3 In what ways do we use a lot of plastic?
4 Why do you think people use so many plastic bags?
5 Do you think schools should recycle more?

7.1

1

A: I've got this new rucksack which is perfect for going camping.

B: Oh great! That'll be handy for our trip in the summer.

2

A: Max can't find the photo he needs for his passport.

B: I think I saw it on top of the fridge.

3

A: I'm so sorry I'm late. Why can I never be on time?!

B: It's okay, you're only a minute late. I know a boy who always arrives ten to fifteen minutes late. That drives me mad!

4

A: So, we went to a restaurant where you can eat as much as you want for twenty euros!

B: Really? Where is it? I'd love to go!

5

A: There's a boy in my class who speaks five different languages.

B: Five? That's amazing!

6

A: The sightseeing trip my dad booked was brilliant.

B: Was it? What did you see?

7

A: Anna enjoyed the trip her friends organised for her birthday.

B: Did she? Oh, that's great. It was such a lovely surprise for her.

8

A: We stayed in a very small town where everyone knew each other.

B: Sounds lovely for a holiday, but I wouldn't want to live there.

AUDIOSCRIPTS

7.2

1 Where's your passport? You haven't forgotten it, have you?

2 We can't check in until later, so let's go and get a coffee.

3 We've been stuck in this traffic jam for an hour now. It feels like forever!

4 The plane's going to take off in a minute, so I have to turn my phone off. I'll call you when I arrive. OK, yeah … speak to you later. Bye!

5 How long will we be on the motorway for? Can we stop and get a drink?

6 Dad should be here soon. His plane lands in ten minutes.

7.3

1 the bags you carry when travelling

2 a place where people, especially young people, stay for a short time at a low cost

3 when a hotel provides guests with three meals a day

4 an underground train system

5 a holiday on a large ship

6 a document an airline gives you so that you can get onto a plane

7 a holiday where you stay somewhere that has a kitchen, and you make your own meals

8 the system of money a country uses

7.4

1 Go to our YouTube channel to see videos about our travels in southern Europe.

2 In each video, we present interesting places that you might one day explore.

3 We interview backpackers to find out what they think about the regions they've visited.

4 We research food in the area and tell you all about it.

5 To catch our next episode, visit our channel on the twenty-seventh of June.

6 Our episodes are all approximately thirteen minutes in length.

7.5

Hi. I'd like to tell you about my online travel show, A Teenager's Travels. It aims to show people the beauty of different cultures. I loved travelling from a really young age. I was about six when I first took a trip away. However, I didn't start filming my experiences until I was twelve. Now I'm eighteen, I can say that I'm quite an experienced blogger!

My very first video was of me in the middle of Scotland. The castle we were visiting was lovely but I can't say the same about the quality of the video! I've certainly improved my filming skills since then. I've also visited all kinds of amazing places. My favourite was filming from the top of a mountain but I've also filmed in a rainforest, national park and many other places.

When I started out, I mostly travelled with my parents because, obviously, I was young and they were paying! My cousin usually came too because I don't have any brothers or sisters and my parents wanted me to have someone my age with me. Nowadays I tend to travel with a friend.

To make my travel show interesting, I have to travel to several different places every year. Deciding where to go isn't easy. There are a lot of travel websites online that tell you about popular places at the moment, but I prefer blogs because then I can find out about cool places from travellers before they become popular!

I learn so much when I travel. I learn about geography, for example. I can name most countries in the world! The most exciting thing for me, though, is history. I love imagining what life was like in different places a century or more ago.

I also make sure I meet people who live in the area because they can teach me and the people who watch my show a lot. If they're really interesting, I'll put an interview with them in my film. It's good for my fans to hear what they have to say. They can see the world through their eyes and not just mine.

7.6 and 7.7

E = Examiner   G = Girl   B = Boy

E: Mariam, do you prefer to travel by plane or by train?

G: Erm, well, I've never been on a plane, so I can't really answer that! I've been on a train lots of times and it's usually enjoyable. Sometimes it can be very crowded, though, so I don't enjoy it then.

E: What about you, Ben?

B: Unlike Mariam, I've been on a plane. I think I prefer flying because it's faster than a train. Also, when you fly, you usually go to a different country, which is more interesting. When I travel by train, it's usually to another town or city nearby.

E: Mariam, which is more fun: going to the beach or going to the mountains?

G: I think going to the beach because there are more things to do there. You can swim in the sea or visit a water park or something. There isn't so much to do in the mountains.

E: Ben, what about you?

B: As Mariam said, there are lots of things to do at the beach but it depends on the month. In the winter, the mountains are better because you can go skiing. You can't really do much at the beach in winter. It's too cold.

7.8

1

A: A common problem is that people lose their luggage on their flight. It happened to my grandparents once.

B: That's never happened to me, but our flight was delayed last year and we had to sit in the airport for eight hours.

2

A: The best holiday I've ever had was at a campsite near a river. I learnt how to fish and then cook the fish on the barbecue.

B: I've never done that. My favourite holiday was to Venice. I loved all the old buildings there. It was really beautiful.

3

A: When I'm bored on holiday, I watch a film on my phone or tablet if I can.

B: Like Eva, I watch a film, or I read a book. I usually have some books on my phone.

4

A: People go on holiday to relax for a week or two. They want to stop thinking about their work and do something fun.

B: I agree with Eva. People get very stressed these days, so they need to relax. Holidays help them to do that.

7.9

1 A common problem is that people lose their luggage on their flight. It happened to my grandparents once.

2 The best holiday I've ever had was at a campsite near a river. I learnt how to fish and then cook the fish on the barbecue.

3 When I'm bored on holiday, I watch a film on my phone or tablet if I can.

4 People go on holiday to relax for a week or two. They want to stop thinking about their work and do something fun.

8.1

1 Am I in the right queue for tickets?

2 Where can I buy a souvenir?

3 What day is it?

4 Do you need your swimming costume?

5 When is your friend going to arrive?

6 Are your parents going to pick you up after the match?

7 Where's your sister?

8 Do you have a phone charger?

8.2

1 Maria

I like it because it's something you can do indoors – you know, when the weather's too bad to actually meet up. We arrange a time and we all connect and interact while we're playing. I find myself talking to the little figures on the screen and sometimes I forget that my friends aren't in the room!

2 Amy

I spend about an hour playing every day. I need to train my fingers to find the right notes without me having to think about it. My teacher says I should do more theory too, but I like playing best!

3 Max

I've got about sixty now. We had to put a special shelf in my bedroom so I can display them all. I buy them online or get them for my birthday or Christmas. Some of my friends do the same and we swap if we get doubles.

4 Daniel

I don't make cakes and biscuits – I prefer things like pies or pasta. I don't always follow a recipe. I add my own ingredients and see what it tastes like. Luckily, my family don't mind if I practise on them!

5 Fred

We're practising a play at the moment. It's quite difficult to learn all the lines but I enjoy rehearsing, and taking on different roles. The play has a few songs in it as well, so I'm practising those at home in the shower!

6 Katie

It suits me because I'm very creative and I'm a patient person – each piece takes a long time. At the moment I'm working on a necklace for my friend's birthday. I found a design online and I'm using beads in her favourite colours.

8.3

1 the thirtieth of May, two thousand and six
2 ten euros ninety-nine cents
3 five and a half thousand
4 eighty percent
5 two point seven five
6 the second of December, nineteen seventy-two
7 four hundred and nineteen
8 thirteen point oh two percent

8.4

N = Narrator

1

N: Which ingredient does the girl need?

A: Have you got everything you need to make the omelettes, Emily?

B: No, I haven't got it all yet. I've got the milk, lots of things to go inside them, and I bought some cheese because I thought you might want to put some on the top.

A: Yes, I will. How many eggs have you got?

B: Well, that's the thing. I think I should get more, because there will be four of us at dinner. I'll go and buy another box.

2

N: What is the boy's hobby?

I used to play online and that's how I learned most of the strategy and got better. There are tutorials which teach you all about the different pieces – the shapes and also how much they're worth in an exchange. But really the game is all about the fight with your rival. It's more fun to play with an actual opponent, not in 'virtual reality'. I play against my cousin every Sunday and we sometimes enter local competitions. I've won twelve matches this season.

3

N: What does the girl need to buy after school?

A: Are you coming to the café with us?

B: No, I need to go to the art shop before it closes. I've got some homework to do tonight.

A: What do you need? Maybe I could lend it to you?

B: Well, I've been painting multi-coloured shapes, and tonight I need to stick them together so they look like a window. I've got thirty-six pieces of paper to stick together, but no glue!

A: Oh. I haven't got any, sorry.

B: Don't worry. I'll get some at the shop and then I'll meet you afterwards.

4

N: Which photo did the girl take at the weekend?

A: Did you enjoy your stay with your aunt and uncle, Lisa?

B: Yeah, it was great. It was good to get some peace and quiet – you know, get away from the town for a while.

A: Yes, I know what you mean. But I think it would be too quiet for you if you lived there. Do you think you'd like to be there three hundred and sixty-five days a year?

B: I'm not sure. But I got some good photos, look! I took this from my bedroom window. Look at the view. So green and not a house in sight!

A: That's a great picture.

5

N: Which instrument does the boy want to learn?

A: So have you decided which instrument you're going to learn?

B: Yes. Well, I thought about the guitar, but everyone plays that, don't they? I want to play something a bit more unusual.

A: But didn't you want to learn the piano?

B: Well, yes, but that's not very unusual either, is it? Besides, I want to learn something that I can carry around and I also want to make progress quickly. So, I think I'll go with the saxophone. Someone told me that if you practise, you can learn it pretty well in two years.

6

N: Where does the girl want to meet Jack on Saturday?

Hi, Jack. Um, I just wanted to let you know what's happening on Saturday. We all need to meet up to work on the history project. So I'm going to the library first with Sarah to get some of the books we need, and then I thought we could meet at my house at about eleven o'clock. It's opposite that new café on Fisher Street. It's number seventy-four. Anyway, I'll text you the address. Can you text me back to let me know you've got the message? See you later. Bye!

7

N: What's the boy most looking forward to doing this weekend?

A: Hey Ash, what are you doing this weekend?

B: Well, my cousins are coming to stay so tomorrow we're walking up to the top of Pike's Hill with a picnic.

A: Oh, great!

B: Then, on Sunday morning we're having a family basketball game down at the park. I really can't wait for that. I love beating my cousins.

A: Sounds fun. Do you know what time you'll be there? I might come and watch.

B: Probably about eleven. After that, we'll have a big family meal at home. I expect we'll fight over the food. We usually do but it'll be nice.

8.5

1 That sounds great.
2 I'm not sure.
3 How about doing some online gaming this evening?
4 Shall I book a room so we can practise?
5 I like the idea, but I'm busy tomorrow.
6 Why don't we try using a zoom lens?
7 That's a good idea.
8 Would you like to have the first turn?

8.6

A: OK, so we need to finish building this today and we only have two hours. How about asking Ryan and Emma to help?

B: I'm not sure about that. I'd rather we worked it out ourselves.

A: OK. Why don't we look in the manual again and go back through each step in the instructions?

B: That's a great idea. Then we can see if we have missed anything.

A: Shall I check we've got all the pieces while you read aloud?

B: Agreed. I'll read and you check. And I'll tick each instruction as we check it.

A: Yes, OK. This all sounds like a good idea. Let's see if it works!

8.7 and 8.8

A: Right, we need to choose a course for the girl to do in the holidays. Would you like to start?

B: Yes, thanks. How about the computer course – learning coding, perhaps? I think it would be interesting to know how to program a computer.

A: Hmm … I'm not sure about that. It wouldn't be very interesting to do it every day over the holidays. What about learning chess? Playing matches would be fun.

B: Um, I don't think chess is a good idea. I tried playing with my cousin once and we both hated it. I'd rather choose something that's more popular with people our age. How about learning the guitar?

A: Yes, a musical instrument is a nice idea, but she may prefer something she can make progress in. I don't think she can learn to play the guitar in such a short time.

B: Yes, you're right. Why don't we recommend something more creative, then? Painting is creative, but I think it's for older people. So what about the creative writing course?

A: Yes, that's a good idea. It's interesting, creative and it could also help her with her school work.

B: Great! So shall we choose the creative writing course?

A: Yes, let's go with that.

8.9

1 Shall we suggest the creative writing course?
2 What about the computer course?
3 How about recommending the art course?
4 Why don't we suggest the guitar course?
5 What about the jewellery-making course?

8.10

1 That's a great idea. It's creative and can be very useful.
2 That's a nice idea, but a fun or creative activity might be better for the summer holidays.
3 That sounds a bit boring. I'd prefer to choose something a bit more exciting.
4 That sounds great! It's creative, relaxing and fun.
5 I'm not sure about that. Jewellery-making is very expensive, isn't it?

9.1

We had a really great vacation in London. I was pretty nervous before we went, because I had never flown to another country before. There are plenty of great places to visit in our country, so we had only been on vacation in the US before. So that meant we all had to get passports. We were happy that they had just arrived in time for the trip – a couple of days before we got the plane.

Anna's family let us use their car while we were in London, which was great. But my parents took it slow at the beginning – they had never driven on the left before. Oh, and I almost got into an accident because I hadn't thought that crossing the street would be different! You have to look right first, then left. But I got it after the first day.

I think the best thing about London was all the super-old buildings. I loved them – especially Buckingham Palace. I had never seen a real palace before that.

9.2

1 OK, don't worry. We can catch the next bus. So, I'll check the timetable on my phone.

2 What a shame! I was really looking forward to that film and it wasn't what I expected. It feels like we wasted our time.

3 I'm not sure I've done enough work. I think I'm going to forget the answers at the last minute. Where's my lucky pencil?

4 I feel terrible. I didn't even say 'happy birthday'. She made me that beautiful card for my birthday. I'm such a bad friend.

5 And why did Catherine get a higher mark than me? My project was just as good. I deserve to get an 'A' as well.

6 We've practised the scene lots of times, so I'm sure we'll be fine. It's going to be the best play we've ever done and people are going to love us!

9.3

A: I think I'm ready for the hiking trip. Are you?

B: No, I haven't finished packing yet. What do you think I should take?

A: Well, Mr Blackburn said that we ought to wear shorts and boots, but also take a hat and sunglasses with us. It can be cloudy in the mountains, but it will still be hot.

B: OK. Shall I take my guidebook so we won't get lost?

A: I wouldn't if I were you. Remember, we've got to carry everything and that book is really heavy! I think they'll give us maps of the area when we get there.

B: Why don't you take the compass you got for your birthday, then? We can practise orienteering.

A: Good idea.

9.4

N = Narrator

1

N: You will hear two friends talking about an exchange programme.

A: I still haven't decided what to do about the French exchange.

B: You haven't signed up yet? I have.

A: I'm not sure about being away from home. I've never been abroad.

B: Did you talk to Mrs Weston about it?

A: Yes, I did. She said it would be good for me to practise speaking. She says I'll forget all about home once I get there.

B: Why don't you ask your parents what they think? And your sister? Didn't she do the French exchange two years ago?

A: Yes, she did. That's a good idea.

2

N: You will hear a boy telling a friend about a course he did.

A: How was the windsurfing course?

B: It was good, thanks.

A: Did you get a certificate at the end?

B: No, but they did have a ceremony with medals on the last day. Some people were a bit embarrassed to stand up in front of everyone, but I didn't mind.

A: So, you did well.

B: Yeah. I was proud that I managed to stand on the board and even sail for a bit. It's not easy.

A: I know – you need to have really strong arms.

B: Yes, it's quite tiring.

3

N: You will hear a girl talking to her brother about a problem she is having with a friend.

A: I don't know what to do about Maria. She's really jealous that I won the science prize.

B: How do you know?

A: Well, yesterday she told me to stop talking about it. She said she was bored with hearing about it.

B: Don't listen to her. I think you should be proud of winning.

A: Thanks. Maybe I will ask the teacher not to display the prize in class, though.

B: I wouldn't do that if I were you. You don't need to be ashamed of doing well. Don't worry, Maria will get over it!

4

N: You will hear two friends talking about an event they attended.

A: I'm glad to be home, aren't you? I really need to get some sleep.

B: Me too. I mean, the music was great, but the camping part was really uncomfortable. It spoiled the event for me.

A: Yes, I know. Next time we should take an inflatable mattress, not mats.

B: Yeah, good idea. I think we ought to take ear plugs too if we go again. And we forgot to take a torch.

A: And we really needed one.

B: Never mind. Next year we should be experts at camping!

5

N: You will hear a boy talking to a friend about doing chores at home.

A: Sorry I'm late. I had to clean the car.

B: That's OK. Do you always clean the car?

A: Yes, but I don't mind. At least it isn't as boring as vacuuming. That's what my sister has to do.

B: I help a bit at home, but we aren't organised like your family – we just do stuff when it needs doing. My parents say that young people should do chores – you know, to learn to be responsible at home.

A: The problem is, when do you get it all done?

B: I know. I've got homework and gymnastics as well. I'm always busy!

6

N: You will hear two friends talking about a football match.

A: So, it's the semi-final on Saturday. How are you feeling?

B: I'm quite relaxed, actually. I'm surprised that I'm not more worried!

A: Didn't you lose to this team last season?

B: We did. But we're a much better team now. We've done loads of extra training. The coach made us practise corners for an hour yesterday. Some boys were complaining that it was boring, but I think we needed to do it.

A: So you feel ready?

B: Yeah. I'm looking forward to it.

9.5 and 9.6

A: So we have to choose an activity that teenagers would enjoy.

B: Well, what do you think about playing in a band? I think they would enjoy it because it's creative.

A: I'm not sure. Everyone likes listening to music, but maybe they can't all play music with other people. How about a virtual reality game? It would be exciting.

B: I'm sorry, I don't agree. I think some of the group would find it boring. Maybe they would prefer to do something outdoors.

A: They could go hiking. Being out in the countryside is relaxing. And you can chat – it's sociable.

B: Yes, hiking sounds good, but I don't think it will be a new activity for all of them. We need to choose something for the group to try for the first time.

A: What about horse-riding? Not many people go horse-riding.

B: I'm not sure that's a good idea. It's quite expensive, isn't it?

A: Yes, you're right. Well, they could try judo.

B: Hmm … But they can't do that all together – they have to do it in pairs.

A: I see what you mean. And some people might not like fighting anyway.

B: How about badminton, then? It's a bit different.

A: Yes, it is. Four people can play badminton together. And it's not too expensive.

B: I agree. Let's choose badminton.

9.7 and 9.8

1 I'm into sport so I do karate once a week after school, I usually play tennis most days in the summer, and I'm keen on cycling too. I go cycling with my brother at the weekend.

2 I love karate. I'd say it's because there are lots of special moves to learn, and I also like moving up from one colour belt to the next.

3 I'm not very keen on doing competitions because I think that sport should be mostly about enjoying yourself. And keeping fit, of course.

4 I can't stand team sports. I tried playing football in the school team and I didn't like it. You have to remember to stay in one position and sometimes you can feel that people are disappointed with the way you are playing. I prefer to do sports by myself.

5 Yes, I quite like trying new things. I went canoeing as part of a school trip once and it was a good experience. If you don't try something new, you won't know if you like it.

6 I'm not sure. I don't like heights very much. I don't think I would put myself in a dangerous situation because I'd be worried about getting hurt. It doesn't sound like fun to me.

9.9

1 I'm really into team sports.

2 I generally prefer doing indoor sports.

3 I absolutely love learning new skills.

4 I can't stand doing the same thing every weekend.

5 I'm not very keen on water sports.

6 I'd like to do a bungee jump one day.

10.1

N = Narrator

1

N: Which job does the boy want to do?

A: You know so much about animals. Are you going to train to be a vet?

B: No, I don't think so. I really want to work outdoors but I don't want to study at university for years. I'd like to be a farmer. I saw a TV programme about it. It's hard work but I think I'd love the way of life.

A: Yes. I think you'd be good at it, too.

B: Thanks.

2

N: Where did the girl get her new bag?

A: Cool bag. Did you get it from that new bag shop on the High Street?

B: It's nice, isn't it? No, my aunt made it for me.

A: Really?

B: Yes, she's making lots of them and then she's going to sell them on a stall at the market. It's going to be her new job. But she made this one specially for me as a present.

A: Wow!

3

N: What is the prize for the winner of the radio competition?

So, don't forget that Friday is the last day to send us your entries for the 'Top Ten Films' competition. All you need to do is write a list of your favourite ten films of all time. It doesn't matter if you've seen them at the cinema or watched them many times on DVD. Whoever matches the top ten chosen by our film experts wins a copy of the book *Film Favourites of the Twenty-first Century*. Don't forget to include your name, an email address or mobile phone number so we can contact you. And good luck!

4

N: Which activity has the girl just done?

A: How did it go, Julia?

B: It was a good session. I think we're working together much better now. It's difficult, though – the music is fast and we all have to do each move at exactly the same time. But I think we're looking good.

A: Do you feel ready for the show next week?

B: Nearly. I'm glad we're going to do the routine one more time at the dress rehearsal, though. And that's when we'll get to hear the band that's playing for us, which is exciting!

A: I can't wait to see it!

5

N: Which is the last lesson before the school holidays?

A: I can't believe it's nearly the summer holidays.

B: Yeah, I know. No more science lessons until September!

A: What do you mean? We've got chemistry before we go home this afternoon!

B: Oh, have we? I thought we were going to watch the Year 12 drama group.

A: No, we need to finish our experiments from last week.

6

N: Where is the boy at the moment?

Hi, Mum. I'm on the train. I'm phoning to say that I'll be home at about seven o'clock. I'm on the later train because there was a long queue at the ticket office. I missed the six o'clock train. Then I had to wait for a while on the platform. Anyway, can you come and collect me? I'll wait outside the station.

7

N: When does the girl have a job interview?

A: I'm a bit nervous about the interview. It's my third interview this month.

B: The one for the Saturday job? Don't worry, you'll be fine. When is it?

A: Well, it was on the thirtieth but they called me last week and changed the date. So it's tomorrow, the thirteenth.

B: Oh! Unlucky for some!

A: Don't say that, Dad!

B: Sorry! I'm sure you'll get the job.

10.2

N = Narrator

8

N: You will hear two friends in a shop looking at mobile phones.

A: That's the phone my cousin's got.

B: The silver one with the big screen?

A: Yes, that's the one. He says a screen like that is great because it's big enough for watching films and stuff.

B: Hmm … I guess it's expensive.

A: Not too expensive for what it does.

B: It's quite ugly, though, isn't it?

A: Yes, it is.

9

N: You will hear two friends talking about a problem at school.

A: I'm worried about the homework I handed in yesterday.

B: Why?

A: I copied the idea from Gemma. It wasn't my own work. I'm sorry I did it.

B: Oh dear! I remember when something like that happened to me. I felt bad afterwards. I kept thinking about it all the time.

A: I know. What did you do?

B: Well, I told the teacher in the end. I think you ought to be honest, too.

A: Yes, you're probably right.

10

N: You will hear two friends who are lost.

A: This isn't the right way. I think we're lost.

B: Oh dear! It's getting late. Do you think we should stop the next person we meet and ask them the way?

A: I'm not sure. We haven't seen anyone else for ages. We can't keep walking away from the route!

B: How about calling your mum and dad?

A: We can't because there isn't a phone signal here.

B: Why don't we go back to that sign we saw with the map on it? Then we can see exactly where we are.

B: Great idea.

11

N: You will hear a girl talking to a friend about her holiday.

A: Did you have a good holiday?

B: Yes, thanks. I didn't think I would enjoy camping so much, but I did. We stayed near a national park, and the scenery was really beautiful.

A: Was it a big campsite?

B: No, it was quite small and not great, to be honest. The showers didn't work for two days and it was a bit noisy at night.

A: Who did the cooking?

B: Mainly my dad. He's not very good at cooking, though! I was just happy to eat outside, with the mountains in the distance. I felt really close to nature.

12

N: You will hear a brother and sister talking about studying for exams.

A: How is the revision going?

B: OK, I suppose. I find some subjects more difficult than others, and I never want to spend much time doing those ones.

A: I remember that from when I was revising. You need to set yourself a goal – you know, say, 'If I do ten exercises on this topic, I can have half an hour playing on the computer.'

B: Good idea, but I'm not sure I can do that. I need someone else to push me to study, really.

A: Well, why don't you call your friends and see if they want to meet up and study with you? You could meet three times a week and study a different subject each time.

B: Yes, I'll try that, thanks.

13

N: You will hear two friends talking about babysitting.

A: Why didn't you come to the cinema last night?

B: I was babysitting my little brothers.

A: Oh. I sometimes babysit for my parents. It's fun but it's difficult to get the kids to go to bed. It gets later and later, and they get really tired.

B: Yes, I know what you mean. I like doing it, but I wish my parents gave me some money for it. It's hard work!

A: You're right. If our parents got someone else to do it, they would have to pay, wouldn't they?

B: Yes! Well, I'm going to talk to my parents about it.

10.3

Cooking was my first love and I still really enjoy my job at the restaurant. Any chef will tell you that you can't work in a kitchen if you don't love your job. It's often really hard work and it's not easy to get a well-paid job. I worked my way up from the bottom, you might say. Because when I left school, I started by washing dishes at my local restaurant.

It's difficult to say how long it takes to train to be a chef because it depends how you get there. In my case, it was five years before I was in charge of a kitchen. It can happen quicker if you go to catering college. Courses take about two years, but I needed to earn money, so I started work and learned as much as I could every day.

There's more to being a chef than people think. Of course, you have to prepare food, cook it and get it ready for the customers – make sure it looks perfect on the plate. But I'm in charge of ordering ingredients, too. It's a lot of responsibility to make sure we don't run out of anything.

My working hours are not great. I really need more time off, but chefs have to work evenings, weekends and holidays. Those are the times when people want to go out and eat! I must start early in the morning and I often finish at midnight. Having a car is essential because there's no public transport that late at night.

Another disadvantage of the job is the wages. You don't earn a lot unless you're able to run your own restaurant or be a head chef. But there are some great reasons to become a chef. One is that a chef can travel. The skills you need to prepare food are very similar in any country, so if you want to see the world, it would be a great career for you.

I thought about being a private chef for a while, cooking for a celebrity on a huge country estate. That was my dream, along with being a food stylist, working on the food you see in photographs in recipe books. What I'd love to do next, though, is to cook on a cruise ship. It would be a fantastic way to travel while I work.

10.4

I = Interviewer   A = Amy

I: Hi, Amy. Thanks for talking to us about your career in nursing. Can I ask you if you always wanted to be a nurse?

A: Yes, I did. It's strange because no one in my family worked in a hospital, and biology wasn't my favourite subject at school. I just knew that I wanted to do good in my job, you know? To help others.

I: Do you remember your first day at work?

A: Yes, of course, although it was many years ago! I remember that I couldn't wait to begin. I wanted to put my training into practice. I didn't really have time to worry on that day because it was really busy, like every day since!

I: And how do feel about being a nurse now, after all these years?

A: Most of the time I'm very happy at work. Sometimes I get frustrated and angry because people come to hospital when they don't really need to. I have to spend my time treating them when there are more urgent cases. The more people that come, the longer others have to wait – sometimes hours and hours. But I have to be polite and treat everyone the same.

I: What do you enjoy most about being a nurse?

A: Well, I like working with my colleagues and meeting different people every day. But I'd say the best thing about the job is helping people. The feeling when you save someone's life is amazing. There's no other way I can describe it.

I: And how do you see the next ten years of your career as a nurse?

A: I love the challenges of my department, so I don't think I'm going to move. I am already a nurse specialist, but I could train to be a nurse consultant. I'm not keen on that idea, because it would mean less contact with patients. I'm going to keep helping people every day. It gives me a lot of job satisfaction.

I: Amy, what would you say to anyone who is thinking about becoming a nurse?

A: You have to be prepared to go to university, so you have to like studying and you have to be very good at getting on with people – I mean your colleagues *and* the public. I would recommend doing some voluntary work or getting a part-time job where you care for other people. Do it before you apply to university, so you can see if nursing is really for you.

I: That's great advice, Amy. Thank you.

10.5

What's your name?

Where do you come from?

What subjects do you study at school?

Thank you.

10.6

How do you get to school every day?

What did you do last weekend?

Do you think that English will be useful for you in the future? Why or why not?

Thank you.

10.7

Now I'd like you to talk on your own about something. I'm going to give you a photograph and I'd like you to talk about it. Here is your photograph. It shows young people studying together. Please tell us what you can see in the photograph.

10.8

Now, in this part of the test you're going to talk about something together for about two minutes. I'm going to describe a situation to you.

A girl doesn't know what job she wants to do when she leaves school. She likes maths and science. She's very intelligent and she likes studying. Here are some pictures of jobs she could do. Talk together about the different jobs and say which would be best.

All right? Now talk together.

10.9

Have you started to think about a career yet?

Why is it sometimes hard to choose a job to do?

Is it a good idea for everyone to go to university or college? Why or why not?

Are there jobs that are only for women or only for men?

Thank you. That is the end of the test.

The *Cambridge English Qualification B1 Preliminary for Schools Exam*, otherwise known as *Cambridge Preliminary for Schools*, is set at B1 level of the Common European Framework of Reference for Languages (CEFR). It has four separate papers: Reading, Writing, Listening and Speaking. Each paper carries 25% of the marks.

Reading: 45 minutes
Writing: 45 minutes

Listening: 35 minutes (approximately)
Speaking: 12 minutes for

All the examination questions are task-based. Rubrics (instructions) are important and should be read carefully They set the context and give important information about the tasks. All the tasks in the exam, and all the texts you read and listen to, have been specially chosen to reflect the interests and experience of school-age learners of English.

Paper	Formats	Task focus
Reading 6 tasks 32 questions	**Part 1:** multiple-choice Reading five separate short texts and answering one multiple-choice question about each text.	Reading to understand the main message.
	Part 2: multiple-matching Reading descriptions of five people and matching each to one of eight short texts.	Reading to understand specific information and the detailed meaning of descriptions.
	Part 3: multiple-choice Answer five multiple-choice questions about a text from four options.	Understanding of the detailed meaning of the text and attitude/opinions of the writer.
	Part 4: gapped text Choosing sentences to fit into the gaps of a text, with a total of six sentences to place correctly.	Reading to understand how texts are organised and sentences relate to each other.
	Part 5: multiple-choice cloze Choosing the missing word for six gaps from a choice of four listed after the text.	Reading to understand particular words and phrases and use of words for creating meaning.
	Part 6: open cloze Choosing which word is needed to fill each gap in a short text. Six gaps in total.	Reading to understand sentence construction and how words/ phrases relate to each other.
Writing 2 tasks	**Part 1:** email Writing an email of 100 words in reply to a text, covering the points in that text.	Focus on writing an email in an appropriate style and responding to the input text.
	Part 2: longer piece of continuous writing Producing one story or article of 100 words.	Writing using a range of language, creating a well organised text in a particular style.
Listening 4 tasks 25 questions	**Part 1:** visual multiple-choice Seven short recordings, each with a multiple-choice question.	Understanding specific information and detailed meaning.
	Part 2: multiple-choice Six short recordings with one multiple-choice question for each.	Understanding gist, ideas and opinions and agreement/ disagreement.
	Part 3: sentence or note-completion Completing six gaps in a set of sentences/ notes, with words, numbers, or names.	Listening and recording specific information.
	Part 4: multiple-choice Answering six multiple-choice questions about an interview	Understanding detailed meaning of the interview, including the attitudes and opinions.
Speaking 4 tasks	**Part 1:** introduction (2–3 minutes) Answering questions from the examiner about yourself.	Giving personal information, social conversation.
	Part 2: describing a photograph (1 minute each) Individual description of a given photograph.	Using appropriate vocabulary,, organising language to describe what you see.
	Part 3: collaborative Task (2–3 minutes) Two-way conversation between candidates about a task with visual prompts	Maintaining a conversation, responding to others, giving suggestions, discussing alternatives, giving reasons. reasons for your opinions.
	Part 4: discussion (3–4 minutes) Discussion of questions asked by the examiner.	Giving opinions on a range of issues, explaining reasons.

Pearson Education Limited

KAO TWO,
KAO Park
Hockham Way,
Harlow, Essex,
CM17 9SR
England
and Associated Companies throughout the world. pearsonELT.com/goldexperience

© Pearson Education Limited 2019

pearsonELT.com/goldexperience

First published 2019
Eighteenth impression 2024

ISBN: 978-1-292-19464-6

Set in Camphor Pro

Printed in Slovakia by Neografia

Acknowledgements
Written by Lucy Frino and Lindsay Warwick. The authors and publishers would like to
thank the first edition authors, Jill Florent and Suzanne Gaynor, for their contribution
to this work.

The Publisher and author would like to thank Nick Kenny for his feedback and
comments during the development of the material.

Picture Credits
*The publisher would like to thank the following for their kind permission to reproduce
their photographs:*

(Key: b-bottom; c-centre; l-left; t-top)

123RF.com: Andrey Armyagov 39, Andriy Popov 39, Artisticco LLC 23, Bonzami
Emmanuelle 73, Iosif Lucian Bolca 50, Lorelyn Medina 22, Maksym Bondarchuk 73,
Marina Zlochin 34, Rafal Olkis 61, Sergii Gnatiuk 39, Vereshchagin Dmitry 39, Zoia
Lukianova 73, daisydaisy 72, somrak jendee 39; **Alamy Stock Photo:** Blend Images 18,
Cultura Creative (RF) 6, FMC 30, 86, Findlay 45, Gruffydd Thomas 76, Image Source 86,
Kevin Britland 24, Konstantin Kopachinskiy 4, Marcin Rogozinski 64, Martin Wierink
73, Matt Limb OBE 37, ONOKY - Photononstop 30, Prisma by Dukas Presseagentur
GmbH 61, Tracy Daniel 42, Westend61 GmbH 54, 58, 6, Weyo 69, XiXinXing 37, flavia
raddavero 32, imageBROKER 11, itanistock 58, mauritius images GmbH 36; **Getty
Images:** Daisy-Daisy 32, Ed Bock 46, Inti St Clair 8, John M Lund Photography Inc 67,
Jose Luis Pelaez Inc. 32, Juanmonino 30, Jupiterimages 33, Jupiterimages / Brand X
Pictures 98, Maskot 10, Ranta Images 32, 62, Sol de Zuasnabar Brebbia 38, TopVectors
47, Vinit Deekhanu / EyeEm 32, Wavebreakmedia 13, goir 63, shutterjack 41; **Pearson
Education Ltd:** Jon Barlow 86, Jules Selmes 58, 58, 6, 6; **Shutterstock.com:** Aliaksei
Kruhlenia 78, Baishev 45, Brainsil 30, Christine Glade 86, David Pereiras 52, David Steele
4, Faber14 28, FlyingFifeStudio 66, Galina Barskaya 35, GoodMood Photo 45, Hnong
Naja 80, Iakov Filimonov 19, Images By Kenny 61, LightField Studios 6, Marcio Jose
Bastos Silva 73, Milos Muller 61, Monkey Business Images 56, 56, 86, NAPA 65, Nata-Lia
73, Natalia Hubbert 20, Nataly Studio 45, New Africa 60, Richard Whitcombe 49, SFC
61, Tuzemka 56, Vasyl Syniuk 5, chrisbrignell 39, cigdem 45, federicofoto 16, guteksk7
59, kpboonjit 13, muratart 61, reptiles4all 57, sirtravelalot 6, sylv1rob1 58, turtix 75.;

Cover Image: Shutterstock.com: A_Lesik, diy13

Illustrated by:

Clonefront (Beehive Illustration) pp. 9; Carl Morris (Beehive Illustration) pp. 43; Daniel
Limon (Beehive Illustration) pp. 26; 70; Dusan Pavlic (Beehive Illustration) pp. 27, 94,
95; Matt Ward (in the style of Simon Rumble) (Beehive Illustration) pp. 53, 71, 79, 99.

All other images © Pearson Education